SOURCES OF TRANSFORMATION

Sources of Transformation

Revitalizing Christian Spirituality

EDITED BY EDWARD HOWELLS
AND PETER TYLER

continuum

Contents

Preface

The most famous transformation in the New Testament is the Transfiguration (*metamorphosis/transfiguratio*) of Jesus, traditionally on Mount Tabor. The Transfiguration is one of the biblical events most often referred to by Christian mystics. For over a millennium in the East, as well as later in the West, it has even been accorded its own feast. As recorded in the Synoptics (Mt. 17.1-13, Mk 9.2-13, Lk. 9.28-36), the glorious appearance of the Lord to Peter, James, and John took place on the way to Jerusalem before the Passion, so we might think of it not so much as a real change or a new stage in Jesus' life, but rather as the manifestation of what was already there—Christ's divine nature hidden within his humanity. But this may not be accurate. Many modern scriptural scholars have argued that the Transfiguration is actually a post-Easter event that was misplaced in the writing of the Gospels. This would suggest that Jesus appeared in his transfigured glory only after, not before, he had been transformed by the ultimate test of death. His obedience to his Father's will needed to be seen through to the end before he manifested his transformed self to his followers. Without the cross there is no metamorphosis.

If this be the case, it has a valuable lesson for all those concerned with spiritual transformation, the subject of this collection of essays. Briefly put, it suggests that spiritual transformation is always a process rather than a state to be attained, at least as far as this life is concerned. It is a life-long condition of growing: a vocation, a task, a journey with many windings and ups and downs. The itinerary will only be completed to texts, especially literary classics, has within it a capacity to function as a channel of grace. Still, close reading and devout application of spiritual classics has a special role in mediating meaning and enhancing transformation, as Gerald O'Collins shows in his analysis of how Anthony de Mello, a modern spiritual master, enriches our understanding of Ignatius of Loyola's *Spiritual Exercises*. Lives and lifestyles as examples for admiration, and sometimes even imitation, can also be important sources for ongoing transformation. Bernadette Flanagan's essay on the early Irish saint Moninne/Darerca and contemporary women who have chosen the path of solitude and silence illustrates the value of such resources.

The nine essays in the second part of the volume reflect on a wide range of sources of spiritual transformation in two main categories: spiritual classics and contemporary experience. The essays on spiritual classics exemplify creative ways in which ancient texts can take on new life to nourish and challenge us in our own work of transformation, while the reflections on experience often address forms of life rejected or marginalized by the narrow views of spirituality so often, alas, present in some aspects of the Christian tradition. Many forms of texts, even those not overtly religious, can be sources of transformation. This collection is designed to offer hope and challenge to all those willing to commit their lives to pursuing the transfiguration/transformation whose goal is not measured by or in this life.

Bernard McGinn

classics of the Christian tradition but on elements of today's culture that are susceptible to an illuminating analysis in terms of these sources. Conversations are developed between the sources and the various circumstances and concerns of today, under the heading of 'transformation'.

'Transformation' is central to Christian spirituality because it is not just where Christians look for spiritual sustenance that informs their spirituality, but also what they do with these sources and how they open themselves to them. It is as much in the manner of appropriation that a source is regarded as 'spiritual' as in what we term its content or subject matter. This is not merely a question of pious attitudes, but of the process of dialogue and engagement with a source by which the 'reader' is transformed. Indeed, sources are judged to be 'spiritual' in Christian spirituality primarily because they have this potential to transform. Accordingly, when we study the sources of spirituality, we are concerned with how they relate to their readers for transformation.

The book begins with James Alison's study of the Lukan account of the giving of the Holy Spirit in the New Testament. Alison focuses on the invitation in the account for the Christian community to discover its identity in the void between Gethsemane and the Resurrection. The 'source' of Christian spirituality is found to be not simply in the past but the ongoing historical reality of a community reading itself in terms of these events, and finding itself within an understanding of the self-giving of the Holy Spirit unleashed in Jesus' death. Far from being an ethereal, insubstantial and a-historical reality, this is an 'anthropological project' of human transformation in relation to the narrated events of Jesus' life and death. Alison builds on this insight to ask questions about the authenticity of the church community that finds its source in these events, at a time when the structures of political and ecclesial authority are undergoing change.

Bernard McGinn turns our attention to the vast range of concerns included in the Christian understanding of humanity as made in the 'image of God'. The 'anthropological project' indicated by Alison, which is begun with the events of the New Testament, is here filled out by reference to the creative contributions of key writers from Christian history. In these sources, humanity is understood to be on a journey of intentional spiritual pursuits. She makes connections with the literature of women solitaries from the past, looking in particular at the example of Darerca or Moninne from the fifth-century Irish context. The conversation between past and present reveals common themes of Christian transformation, such as the movement between solitude and engagement in the community, and the understanding of solitude as helping to restore humanity from the abuses of the world, that is, as a paradoxical form of deepened solidarity with humanity as a whole. By drawing attention to these aspects of transformation, she enriches our understanding of emerging patterns of religious life today, and points out that they extend beyond those who have formal Christian commitments.

In the second part of the book, the chapters are shorter in length and serve to illustrate the wide range of topics that are included in the area of Christian transformation. The first chapters examine traditional Christian texts as sources for the understanding of transformation today. Edward Howells reads Augustine's great speculative work *On the Trinity* as primarily about transformation. Augustine's psychological analogies in the second half of the work are concerned with the growth of human awareness towards contemplation. Scripture and doctrine are used here not merely as external authority but to articulate the inner transformation of the mind. Jeremy Worthen takes up another well-known historical spiritual writer, William of St Thierry, but in a rarely studied text concerning predestination. By comparison with Bunyan's *The Pilgrim's Progress*, he shows that Christian anxiety about predestination is similarly transformed into confident hope, yet by a notably different means in William as compared with Bunyan, reflecting William's pre-modern and less individualist mindset. Michael Plattig, making the Carmelite Rule the topic of his study, brings the Rule into dialogue with modern notions of individuality and solitude, showing that the emphasis on solitary contemplation is best understood within the larger notion of community, rather than as antagonistic to community, thus retrieving an unfamiliar view of solitude for today. Peter Tyler makes an original study of Teresa of Avila's spirituality, examining the connections between her erotic metaphors and the question of bodiliness. There has been an understandable reaction to body–soul dualism in spirituality today, to which Tyler responds instantiated in relation to any part of the world and in every aspect of human experience. This enables Christian writers to see the possibilities for transformation in all kinds of places, both commonplace and marginal, yet as grounded in a single anthropological process. By investigating these sources and turning them towards our own world and time, this book shows their transforming potential in new ways.

There are many people we would like to thank, who have given invaluable help in bringing together this collection. It is not possible to name them all. But, as well as the authors who have given generously of their time, we would like to give special thanks to Dr Michael Hayes (Vice-Principal) and Marie Fernandes at St Mary's University College, whose hospitality and hard work made the initial gathering possible; and to our colleague Br. Patrick Moore of Sarum College who helped us to plan and run the conference.

Edward Howells

Peter Tyler

February 2010

Notes

1   For a good summary of these debates see *Minding the Spirit*, ed. E. Dreyer and M. Burrows (London: Johns Hopkins University Press, 2005), which comprises papers published by the Society for the Study of Christian Spirituality in the United States.

2   For instance, an interest in the question as to whether the study of Christian spirituality is necessarily a 'self-implicating discipline'. See Dreyer and Burrows, *Minding the Spirit*, Part II, 'The Self-Implicating Nature of the Study of Spirituality', pp. 61–152.

3   Published as *With Wisdom Seeking God: The Academic Study of Spirituality*, ed. U. Agnew, B. Flanagan and G. Heylin (Leuven: Peeters, 2008).

PART ONE

Sources of Transformation

1

Befriending the Vacuum:
Transformation and the Sources of
Ecclesial Spirituality

JAMES ALISON

One of the things which fascinates me, as a systematic theologian, and which I have a long-term yearning to understand better, is what is meant by the 'giving' of the Holy Spirit. In John's Gospel we are solemnly assured, at a certain point in Jesus' ministry, 'As yet the Spirit had not been given, because Jesus was not glorified' (Jn 7.39b). In other words, rather contrary to any notions of the Spirit as somehow ethereal, insubstantial, a-historical and so on, what we have is a notion of the Spirit as entering into the human realm in a quite specific historical circumstance and therefore being constantly and ever after shaped by that circumstance. Later in John's Gospel Jesus takes this further when he says that the Spirit: '. . . will glorify me, for he will take what is mine and declare it to you' (Jn 16.14).

What I would like to do in this chapter is to attempt to understand something of what is going on here, and to do so with some help from St Luke.

My hunch is this: that Luke portrays Jesus in between Gethsemane and the Cross as deliberately retracing in historical form the route back from created reality, to being outside of and thus prior to creation. From his prayer of obedience and sweat 'like clots of blood' in which he is the space of death. It is a fully human act. And of course humans cannot fully give themselves away into occupying the space of death with any certainty at all as to what the results of this will be. Or indeed, even as to whether it's a worthwhile thing to do at all. No surrender of control could be greater.

I'd like to look at how this impacts our understanding of Creation. In one sense it's easy, if we follow the imagery of the book of Genesis, to imagine God creating: he creates formless matter and then little by little orders it, and adds things here and there until he rests. We can imagine doing something like that ourselves with respect to clay. The one who does the ordering has, one assumes, a clear idea of what he'd like to make, and moves towards making it.

But the Christian account of creation is somewhat different from this. In the Christian creation story, the Defining Adam, the first giver-of-self-away-in-sacrifice, the first priest, but also the first victim and the first sacrifice, appears in the middle of the story and, with enormous difficulty, gets right what the also-ran Adams, Eves, Cains and Abels, who are all of us, have been getting wrong since the inception of our race, so that Creation really starts with and through the Defining Adam as a human story. And in the Christian account of creation, the Defining Adam is not a passive recipient of YHWH's breath, as the also-ran Adam of Genesis is (cf. 1 Cor. 15.45). The Defining Adam is YHWH as human, and it is YHWH's breath having become a human life story that is breathed into our nostrils so that Creation is in fact a human life story.

What on earth, then, was Jesus thinking? In this account, the relationship between the Spirit and Creation is subtly different from the previous account. Order is not something that comes from without, applied to a formless void. The creative act of both breaching the vacuum into existence and orchestrating its formless void is present simultaneously. If you like, all the energy and emotional push of bringing this project into being, not knowing what it is going to end up like, knowing only that it will zing with joy, has as its analogy not an outside agent moulding clay, but a human offering himself to stand in a place of shameful death so that thoroughly unsatisfactory, as yet incomplete, and often evil humans can ourselves become the agents of Creation, and can become the physical,

This, I think, is one of the great pivots of the cosmic change which has come upon us with the giving of the Holy Spirit: the non-rivalry between the self-giving of Jesus and all the panoply of the forces of death. Because the only conceivable thing (and it is to us scarcely conceivable) that could not be moved by the panoply of the forces of death is something that is prior to life as we know it, and able to hold it in being. In other words, the Spirit which in-formed Jesus' enacted bodily life, and to which Jesus' enacted bodily life gave form, is the Spirit of the Creator, finally detached in our perception from any sort of mistaken identification with death.

I would like to move from my necessarily impressionistic meditation on what Jesus was doing in the 'giving' of the Spirit to looking at the Lukan account of how that 'giving' of the Spirit was received.

We all know the account in Acts 2, nevertheless I would like to give a brief run through part of it to see what Luke is pointing towards:

> When the day of Pentecost had come, they were all together in one place. And suddenly from heaven there came a sound like the rush of a violent wind, and it filled the entire house where they were sitting. Divided tongues, as of fire, appeared among them, and a tongue rested on each of them. All of them were filled with the Holy Spirit and began to speak in other languages, as the Spirit gave them ability. Now there were devout Jews from every nation under heaven living in Jerusalem. And at this sound the crowd gathered and was bewildered, because each one heard them speaking in the native language of each.

First of all, the event is linked to the Passover by occurring on Pentecost, the feast celebrated fifty days after Passover, so whatever happens, it can be seen as in some way completing Passover, with its liberation from Egypt. The apostolic witnesses are all gathered together, and there comes a sound like the rush of a violent breath – πνωη rather than πνευμα – the more personal form 'breath', as in that which God breathed into Adam in Genesis 2 (and the risen Jesus into the disciples in John 20), rather than the yet-to-be-made personal form which hovered over the abyss in Genesis 1.

his death in sharing the portions of himself with his disciples in the Last Supper, just as the High Priest gave portions of the lamb of atonement to the priests in the Temple. But simultaneously, with the fire resting on the heads of those who are receiving the portions, it is clear that they are not only priests in the New Temple, but also living burning offerings.

It is now, I think, that it would make sense to go back and look at Isa. 59.15-21:

> Truth is lacking, and he who departs from evil causes himself to be despoiled. The LORD saw it, and it displeased him that there was no justice. He saw that there was no man, and wondered that there was no one to intervene; then his own arm brought him victory, and his righteousness upheld him. He put on righteousness as a breast-plate, and a helmet of salvation upon his head; he put on garments of vengeance for clothing, and wrapped himself in fury as a mantle. According to their deeds, so will he repay, wrath to his adversaries, requital to his enemies; to the coastlands he will render requital. So they shall fear the name of the LORD from the west, and his glory from the rising of the sun; for he will come like a rushing stream, which the wind of the LORD drives. And he will come to Zion as Redeemer, to those in Jacob who turn from transgression, says the LORD. And as for me, this is my covenant with them, says the LORD: my spirit which is upon you, and my words which I have put in your mouth, shall not depart out of your mouth, or out of the mouth of your children, or out of the mouth of your children's children, says the LORD, from this time forth and for evermore.

This is, evidently, a prophesy of redemption, though it has been fulfilled in a way that no one could have expected: it describes the Lord doing himself what no human seemed to be able to do: avenging, which was always one half of redeeming and atoning. And he is going to come to Zion as Redeemer like a vehement (our old friend βιαιος) stream driven by the wind of the Lord. This is linked with making a covenant and putting a spirit upon people which will issue forth in all speaking the words of the Lord.

bearing witness to a huge and genuinely anthropological earthquake being promoted by a Spirit which hadn't been available before, and which Jesus had made available. This huge genuinely anthropological earthquake has quite specific features: a completely new form of unity for humans is being made available at the instigation of a forgiving human victim who lived as if death were not. This completely new form of unity is universal, it is able to be entered into by people of any nation under the sun, and is in principle not over against any race at all (the final step to this is taken after Peter's interaction with Cornelius in Acts 10). From this Spirit a new form of holiness emerges which is nothing to do with the sacred structures of old, but in which what is truly central is the kenotic self-despoiling living-out of being a priest in the New Temple. This Temple is understood as a new corporate being-together of human bodies. It is human living-out of this which is what enables Creation to be fulfilled and to zing with a lasting joy. All of this has happened in the midst of, and through, a quite specific historical bunch of people, the apostolic witnesses, in a normal, non-magnificent, non-liturgical house, and is made available through their spoken words.

Now, why have I gone on for so long to get to something as simple as saying that the Church is One, Holy, Catholic and Apostolic, which we all know anyhow? And the answer is because I'm afraid that we are so used to hearing those words with an ecclesiastical tinge, that we forget the anthropological earthquake which produces ecclesiality, and of which the ecclesiastical is the necessary but sometimes severely dysfunctional carapace. And it is easy for the word 'spirituality' to become a more or less Gnostic way of abstracting from the corporate, anthropological, historical bringing into being of a new humanity in the face of death which is the indispensably ecclesial dimension of the protagonism of the Spirit.

It is just here, I think, that it is going to be increasingly important for us to think in terms of the creative protagonism of the self-giving dead person. And I mean this somewhat literally. If the picture I have begun to sketch out for you is true, then the gift of the Spirit is already the gift of a certain peaceful, unshaken, unmoved, un-driven being able to occupy the space of death creatively. I'm afraid that I think in silly pictures, but delegation of approval, or disapproval to others, who in the last resort usually cannot give an approval that they do not themselves have, is a failure to accept the fullness of responsible involvement for bringing into being the project.

In other words, it is a failure to be dead enough to receive the creative longing of Christ.

However, if we are dead enough, and are thus unconcerned about success, reputation, able not to resist our being despoiled of these apparently life-giving things, then it is conceivable that we will be able to think big enough, think long-term enough to glimpse the ecclesial form of how the Spirit is befriending the vacuum and bringing Creation into being, and so become the fingertips of its protagonism.

I'd like to conclude with a contemporary example of what I mean, corresponding to elements from two of the 'notes' of the ecclesial project which I mentioned before – its apostolicity and its holiness. Central to the notion of apostolicity, following on the imagery of Acts 2 which I developed earlier, is the link between Word and witness. A certain way of speaking is described, which bore witness to something having been experienced over time, and was picked up by the listeners as something inside them, such that they were able to relate to it, and to its authority from within, from their own starting place. This speaking and listening of itself, as a sign of the Spirit which empowers it, both separates the listeners out from being a crowd, and freshly individuates them by making them symptoms of a new sort of unity. We are talking here about a certain sort of anthropology of communication.

Now one of the things which the last five hundred years have seen, and has advanced dizzyingly in the last few decades, has been an astonishing series of changes in the public use of the Word. From typesetting to Twitter, from papal bulls to popular blogs. And of course, the guardians of the edges (whether secular or religious) are accustomed in this sphere, as in all others, to conserving the forms of the old long after the new wine has burst out and run away. Thanks to the internet people can read things for themselves, disagree with them publicly, find out how others are reacting to them, mock them (often being right to do so) and get an interactive audience such that what it means to speak with authority criers and royal proclamations yielded to newspapers, and once again the appearance of objective truth in the public sphere seemed to grow – even more so with radio, and then television.

However, I wonder whether we haven't entered a new sphere in which the easy interactivity of the published word, the viral spread of information, has severely undercut all the pretensions (for that is all they were – though often enough decent, protective pretensions) of the objectivity of the truth proclaimed by the public holders of the word. I'm not sure whether this is merely a subjective and partisan perception, but I can scarcely begin to fathom the depth of the shock to the possibility of public truthfulness wrought, in the English-speaking world at least, by the eight years between the Florida election of 2000 and the end of the Bush era. I don't merely mean the objective evil wrought by particular individuals within or around the Bush administration and the other governments infected by their lies, or indeed the farcical nature of newspaper and television reporting surrounding these events, or, indeed the systemic mendacity of church authorities which also emerged as never before during this period. I mean the wholesale way in which it became clear that the apparent public bastions of possible truthfulness were little other than factional cheerleaders, champions of convenience, cowards, shameless masters of thuggery and cover-up. This, of course, may always have been the case, to greater or lesser degrees: the anthropological novelty is elsewhere. What is new is that the advent of a non-traditional, interactive, internet-based media means that alternative voices become available with astonishing rapidity – so that official lies can be 'called', however ineffectively, and people can see the shamelessness of liars as they live out their lies, but also that a welter of gossip and conspiracy theories can develop. In other words, what is dramatically altered is not necessarily the amount of truth that is available; the illusion of authority of certain forms of communication is entirely relativized, meaning it is undermined.

Now this, the sense that we may be heading back into being something much closer to an ancient city, riven by misinformation, gossip and factionalized mobs, but with enormous technological advances, cannot but be of huge significance for anyone who is interested in what is meant by dust and to dust you shall return.' There are a series of word games hinted at here around the words for Adam, ground and blood, the Hebrew of all of which have 'dam' at their root.

2 The Hebrew word here translated 'requital' has as its consonants ם ל ש and is linked to the word for peace, completion, settlement by sacrifice: it is one of those genuinely polysemic words surrounding the notion of sacrifice which should by no means always be interpreted as vengeful. My guess is that the τετελεσται – 'it is completed' – of Jn 19.30 is the Greek version of a verbal form of this Hebrew word.

3 I am very grateful to my friend Andrew McKenna for this quote from Anon., *A Woman in Berlin: Eight Weeks in the Conquered City*, trans. Philip Boehm (New York: Picador, 2006), pp. 110–11: 'So the bookseller stitches away and recounts what she knows. Rumor – the goddess Fama. I've always pictured her as an old woman all shrouded up and murmuring away. Gossip. We feed on it. In the old days people got all their news through hearsay and word of mouth. It's impossible to overestimate how this affected ancient cultures, how unclear and uncertain their view of the world must have been – spooky, nightmarish, a swamp of murmured horrors and fears, of malicious men and resentful gods.'

4 Alasdair MacIntyre, *After Virtue: A Study in Moral Theory*, 3rd ed (London: Duckworth, 2007).

5 In his various meditations on Benedictine monasticism and Europe.

6 David Bentley Hart, *Atheist Delusions* (New Haven: Yale University Press, 2009).

2

Humans as Imago Dei: *Mystical Anthropology Then and Now*[1]

BERNARD MCGINN

In 1968 the distinguished Jewish scholar Alexander Altmann published a seminal article under the title "*Homo Imago Dei* in Jewish and Christian Theology," one of the few pieces to pursue this biblical theme from a comparative perspective.[2] Altmann concluded with this observation:

> Merely to speak of the 'dignity of man' without anchoring it in some kind of theology would seem rather futile. Is there a way in which we can once again speak of man as created in God's image without sounding hollow and trivial? Do we still believe in man because we believe in God? The question, it appears, concerns Jews and Christians alike.[3]

Altmann's questions are still with us, perhaps more forcefully than ever, when we consider the contemporary need for theological reflection on the human condition in an age of triumphant secularism, rampant consumerism, and strident religious fundamentalism.

The history of Christian views of theological anthropology, at least down to the Reformation, centered on the belief that humans were created in the image and likeness of God. The biblical basis of this teaching is Gen. 1.26-27, where God says, "Let us make humankind in our image, according to our likeness; and let them have dominion over the fish of narrative of God's creative activity, not only as being located among the "living beings" on the earth (Gen. 1.24-25), but also as created "in the image and likeness of God" (Gen. 1.26). In other Near Eastern religions the ruler often enjoyed the status of being an image of the god of the city or state; only in Israel were all humans accorded this status. But what does this image-nature entail? First of all, the words "image" (*zelem*) and "likeness" (*demut*) should not be conceived of as signifying two different aspects of humanity, but basically as synonyms. The Hebrew terms, unlike many later Christian interpretations, were not intended to distinguish between the inner, or spiritual, dimensions, of the human, and the outer, physical human body. The whole of the human person is God's image and likeness. Second, what ties the original intent of the Yahwist narrative to subsequent readings and interpretations is the fact that image/likeness has always centered on having a special relation to God—human nature, however conceived, has a connection with the divine that exceeds anything else found in the created order.[6] In the words of Gerhard von Rad: "Man is here designated as a creature whose being is not from below but who belongs by nature to the upper region."[7] This unique position is the root of the human command over the animals (Gen. 1.26, 28). There is no question, to be sure, that the Genesis account of humanity's creation in "the image and likeness of God" is anthropocentric. The issue is what kind of anthropocentrism we are dealing with—despotic control, independent manipulation, or responsible stewardship? All these options have been found in the history of Christianity, and are not surprisingly still present today.

In the texts that came to form the New Testament, the theme of God's image plays an important role, especially in Paul.[8] For Paul, Jesus is "the image of the invisible God, the firstborn of all creation; for in him all things in heaven and on earth were created" (Col. 1.15-16; see also 2 Cor. 4.4; Phil. 2.6; Heb. 1.3). Just as the Word incarnate in Jesus Christ was seen as the one through whom creation was made, so too the redemption achieved by Christ on the cross was portrayed as a new creation (see 2 Cor. 5.17-18; Gal. 6.15). Without denying the character of man as image of God given in creation (1 Cor. 11.7; see also Jas 3.9), in this new creation humans receive a renewed or heightened identification with understanding the nature of humanity as image of God: the intellectual, the volitional, and the interpersonal.[11] These three traditions are by no means to be thought of as opposed, or even discrete. Most of the patristic and medieval thinkers who wrote about the nature of humanity have elements of all three, though they usually tend to emphasize one more than the others. The intellectual tradition places the essential nature of the image in man's rational nature as a subject endowed with a reason or intelligence participating in the transcendent divine intellection. As Augustine of Hippo put it in his treatise *On the Trinity*: "Not everything in creatures that is in some way or other similar to God is also to be called his image, but that alone to which he himself alone is superior, for the image is only then an expression of God in the full sense when no other nature lies between it and God."[12] Since mind and reason is what sets man above other creatures and relates it directly to God, the image is essentially found there.

The volitional tradition does not deny that the image is located in the human mind, but it emphasizes human ability to act freely as the core of the *imago dei*. God alone is totally and sovereignly free. The greatest measure of his election of humanity to bear his image consists in the share he gives human beings in this freedom, even to the extent of allowing them to turn away from him in sin, as Adam did. A classic expression of this position is found in Bernard of Clairvaux's treatise *On Grace and Free Choice*.[13] For Bernard, free choice (*liberum arbitrium*) is defined as "a self-determining habit of soul," involving both a spontaneous expression of the will and an accompanying judgment of the intellect. True freedom, of course, is not pure autonomy, but consists in the ability to act freely in accord with the divine freedom. This ability was lost in sin, so that until the coming of Christ all that humans possessed was the truncated freedom from necessity (*libertas a necessitate*), that is, the ability to act without external compulsion, but not apart from an inner inclination to sin (*cupiditas/concupiscentia*). Christ's redeeming act restored the freedom of counsel that enables us to do good and avoid sin (*libertas a peccato*). This exercise of freedom is meant to lead us on to the "freedom from misery" (*libertas a miseria*), the delight that will only be complete in heaven.[14] As Bernard summarizes:

only be understood through contemplation of them in their *logoi*, or higher existence in the divine mind. This perspective helps us understand a second aspect of patristic *imago dei* anthropology. To be made in the image of God is to be made for contemplation (*contemplatio/theôria*), that is, for "deep gazing, attention, vision" into the fundamental reality of the universe (*theôria physikê/contemplatio naturalis*) and even into the incomprehensible nature of God (*theôria theologikê/contemplatio theologica*). To see the human person as fundamentally contemplative is rooted deep in the Greek Fathers, from Clement of Alexandria, through Origen, Evagrius Ponticus, and on into Maximus the Confessor and John Climacus. It is also found among the Latin Fathers, notably in Ambrose, John Cassian, and Gregory the Great. Patristic views of *theôria/contemplatio* utilized a rich tradition of Greek philosophical speculation reaching back to Plato, but the Christian understanding of contemplation, as well as the relation between the effort to attain contemplative vision of higher reality (*bios theôretikos*) and the concrete demands of the active, or practical, life (*bios praktikos*), formed a new stage in the understanding of human nature and destiny.[19]

A third implication of *imago dei* anthropology has to do with what it implies for the unity of humankind. There has been, of course, a certain tension between "insider" and "outsider" views of human nature conceived of as made in the image and likeness of God, both in the Hebrew Bible and in some interpretations of the New Testament. Genesis 1.26-27, as well as other uses of the *imago dei* theme in the Old Testament (e.g. Gen. 5.1-3, and 9.6; Sir. 17.13; Wis. 2.23-24), imply that Adam and all his descendants are created in the image and likeness of God, but the emphasis of the Hebrew Bible on Israel centered on the story of God's chosen people, though some texts in the prophets and Wisdom literature emphasized the universalistic viewpoint in seeing all humans as called by God. In the New Testament the unity of humanity is restored by Christ, God's true image, but there is also a definite ecclesiological aspect to the restoration of humanity's likeness to God.[20] We become more like Christ though our participation in the saving community of the new people of God. Making the notion of image of God an epistemological key for understanding the interaction of Christ and the role of the flesh and soul, like the spirit, were made in God's image. As he puts it in *Against Heresies* 5.9.1:

> Now the soul and the spirit are certainly a part of man, but certainly not the man; for the perfect man consists in the commingling and the union of the soul receiving the Spirit of the Father, and the mixture of that fleshly nature which was also moulded after the image of God. . . . But when the spirit here blended with the soul is united with the body, the man becomes spiritual and perfect because of the outpouring of the Spirit, and this is he who was made in the image and likeness of God.

Other Christian Fathers, such as Origen, were more influenced by Plato and the Platonic tradition; but even these thinkers rejected any simple dichotomy between body and soul and affirmed belief in the resurrection of the body, though understood in different ways.[22] Most patristic authors sought to stress the unity of the human person as a purposefully created body–soul composite, despite their conviction that the image-nature of humanity was primarily realized in the soul or inner person. They adopted various strategies to mitigate the anthropological dualism inherent in Platonism. For example, a number of the Fathers argued that it was a part of humanity's special dignity to have been created with a dual and interdependent nature consisting of body and soul. This teaching, found in Gregory of Nazianzen, reached a high level of theological sophistication in Maximus the Confessor in the seventh century. For Maximus, it is God's will that body and soul come together to form the human person. Although the two elements are independent in principle, their God-given unity is natural and indissoluble—there is no soul without a relation to its body. This union is essential for the redemption of the universe. Maximus insists, ". . . it is out of God's great goodness human beings were composed of body and soul." He continues:

> By practicing the virtues the body gains familiarity with God and becomes a fellow servant of the soul. . . . The result is that what God is to the soul the soul becomes to the body, and the one God,

what was God trying to say by these two words? Some Fathers treated image and likeness as pretty much the same (e.g. Irenaeus), but a greater number identified the image with the inalterable participation with God that could never be lost, even after sin. In this view likeness constituted the dynamic transformative relationship with God that Adam was to have achieved through life in the Garden of Eden, but which only became accessible to humans once again after the coming of Christ. The variations on distinguishing image from likeness were many, sometimes even within the same author. In his *On Grace and Free Choice*, for instance, Bernard of Clairvaux treated *imago* as our permanent relation to God and *similitudo* as the likeness that could be lost and regained, but in his later *Sermons on the Song of Songs* 80–82 he identified both *imago* and *similitudo* as aspects of human nature which partly remain and partly are lost and regained in the course of human history. Bernard was conscious of the variation, remarking that the treatments were *diversa sed non adversa*, that is, "different but not opposed."[26]

Bernard's observation might be applied across the board to image theology. Despite the considerable differences among authors and even within the same author, there is an overall agreement about the basic pattern of this form of theological anthropology that can be expressed under three headings. (1) Humanity was given a unique relationship with God by being created in the divine image and likeness. (2) Through sin, humanity lost important aspects of that relationship, because humans rendered themselves unable to fulfill their calling to become more like God. Finally, (3) the dynamic aspect of the relationship was restored through the Incarnation and Redemption, thus enabling humans to realize their image and likeness nature through a process of growing deification. *Imago dei* anthropology, therefore, is not one thing, but a series of variations on these common themes.

Over the course of the centuries new insights about the relationship between God and humans understood as *imago dei* continued to emerge. The story is so rich that I can do no more than to gesture at a few of the major thinkers who contributed to it. For example, Gregory of Nyssa's treatise *On the Making of Man* presents a meditation on the Genesis creation account that for all its Platonizing elements expresses an original but were also, at least on the level of their virtual pre-existence in God, truly *imago dei*, that is, formally one and the same image as the second person of the Trinity. According to Eckhart, everything that can be said about the Son in the Trinity can also be said about the human intellect *insofar as* it is purely God's image.[30] Hence, as the German Dominican preached, "the eye with which I see God is the same eye with which God sees me."[31] At the end of the fourteenth century Catherine of Siena also stressed the pre-existence of humans in the divine mind, although she used this not for speculation about the soul's identity with God, but as a motivation for recognizing that God has loved us from all eternity: "In holy self-knowledge . . . we see that we were loved before we came into existence, for God's love compelled him to create us in his image and likeness."[32] Catherine's notion of divine love, especially as revealed in her fixation on the redeeming blood of Christ, led her to emphasize the "chain of charity" by which each human being has need of others, so that the test of whether or not one belongs to the saved is the degree to which we love and come to the aid of our neighbor. God tells her: "I have so ordered charity that no one simply enjoys his or her reward in the blessed life that is my gift without its being shared by others."[33]

In the fifteenth century the figure of Nicholas of Cusa represents a distinctive moment in the history of theological anthropology, poised as he is between the Middle Ages and the Renaissance. Cusa's notion of humanity as the "living image of God" (*vivens imago*) both summarizes much of the past and also has a distinctive humanist tone in its stress on the practical form of knowing of the non-clerical and non-monastic world in attaining insight about how to live a full human life. For Cusa human dignity is to become more and more the living image of God in our every form of knowing and acting. The realization of the freedom and responsibility God accords to human beings is emphasized by the divine voice that whispers to the contemplative in chapter 7 of Cusa's mystical treatise *On the Vision of God*, saying, *Sis tuus et ego ero tuus* ("Be yours and I too will be yours").[34]

While it may be true to say that the most creative ages of *imago dei* anthropology ended with the fifteenth century, this central element of Christian thought did not disappear in the centuries that followed. As

I would argue that the core of *imago dei* anthropology's possible importance for today can be summed up under two headings. The first is the threefold relationality entailed in being created in God's image. The human person as image of God is constituted by (1) a relationship to God, (2) a relationship to other humans, and (3) a relationship to the created universe. (These three relationships are constitutive of what it means to be human, and even to be a self, in the sense of having a conscious sense of our identity and dignity.) The second issue involves a more precise delineation of the difference between what I will call "Dignity I" (the dignity given to all humans in their capacity as God's image) and "Dignity II" (the corresponding obligation to act toward a certain end or goal, that is, the duty to responsible exercise of the freedom that flows from the gift of the image).

Christian forms of *imago dei* anthropology conceive of humanity's relationship to God as distinctive among creatures—only humans are formed in the image and likeness of God. Different thinkers have envisaged this relationship in different ways, rooting their views in diverse aspects of human nature, most frequently in the human ability to reason and in human freedom. Among the religions that view humans as created in the image of God, Christians are distinctive in seeing the image as realized on two levels: that of creation and that of redemption. Both stages are conceived of as universal—all humans are descendents of Adam created in God's image and likeness, and all are redeemed from Adam's sin by the Second Adam, Jesus Christ the Incarnate Word, the true *imago dei* and whose coming reveals the full meaning of creation *ad imaginem*, that is, being made "to the image that is to the Word." Many Christian thinkers, like Augustine, take this view a step farther, seeing the image of God as an *imago trinitatis*, an image of the Trinity. Therefore, a serious retrieval of *imago dei* anthropology seems inseparable from a revitalization of a practical trinitarian theology, that is, a deepening realization of the role of the Trinity in both action and contemplation.

Even thinkers who do not share these distinctively Christian conceptions of the *imago dei* on the level of Dignity I may find food for thought in some of the ways Christians have sought to use their understanding of being made to God's image as the foundation for determining the dignity of the human as *imago dei* through purposeful action, has usually been seen as realized primarily in terms of moral obligations, both individual and social. This is the main message of modern papal use of image anthropology, as indeed it should be. Nevertheless, our brief look at some classic analyses of what it means to realize the divine likeness in our lives reveals that moral practice, foundational as it is, is just an initial stage. The higher way of actualizing the image of God in this life is through contemplation. Contemplation is usually understood as a special form of attentive regard toward God. This is true, but contemplative states concentrating on God alone do not rule out, at least for mystics like Meister Eckhart, a more general mode of contemplative life in which heightened attention to all reality becomes the goal of how we should live. When Eckhart says that "The eye with which I see God is the same eye by which God sees me," I do not think that he is only talking about what many would call a religious contemplative vision of God. Rather, he is reminding us that in every sincere act of gazing on the world or on other humans we are seeing God and God is seeing us.

This brings us to the second relationship implied in our status as the image of God, that is, our attitude toward other humans. Once again, I will only lift up two aspects of traditional Christian anthropology that might prove fruitful for further investigation and reformulation. The first is the notion that the truest sense of the *imago dei* is to be found in human nature conceived of as a unity or totality, not as realized in any individual human being who is never more than a particular instantiation of the universal image. Such universalism is found in Gregory of Nyssa and it is present, at least in germ, in a number of other Christian thinkers. The implication of this teaching is that every human has an integral role in the formation of the ultimate dignity of humankind, however much their own actions seem to conflict with this goal. All humans, therefore, should be treated *as if* they are meant to help realize the full and final image of God. This does not, of course, mean we should rule out trying to correct those who consciously reject human dignity, or to continue to resist those who work against the rights of others. We should, however, always attempt to remain conscious of the universal aspect of human dignity.

likeness may also offer food for thought. Of course, the fact that Genesis describes Adam as being given "dominion" over the earth (Gen. 1.27) has been used to excuse people from taking any responsibility for how they treat the earth and care for its resources. Dominion conceived of as a carte blanche to pillage the environment in favor of selfish interests under the banner of God's name is one of the more perverse scriptural misinterpretations of the modern era. Former centuries, which did not possess the technological capability to wreak as much havoc on the planet as we can, did not often advert to this issue. Still, thinkers who reflected on the full meaning of why God bestowed on humans alone the gift of being *imago dei* were conscious that this status involved responsible stewardship, a sense that human beings should always be rational envoys over creation, motivated by their God-given reason and not by the greed and selfishness that were the result of Adam's sin. If the Genesis accounts of the dual creation of humanity can be construed as implying this kind of relation to the planet (see Gen. 1.27 and 2.15), then the re-creation of the image achieved through Christ, which begins the new creation, is in process of being realized not only in human beings (2 Cor. 5.17, Gal. 6.15), but also in the cosmos which Paul describes as "groaning with labor pains" until it "will obtain the freedom of the glory of the children of God" (Rom. 8.21-22). Responsible stewardship of creation, therefore, is an integral aspect of what *imago dei* anthropology invites us to reflect upon as we consider the meaning of human dignity in this new millennium, that is, as we take up once again the question, "What does it mean to be created in the image and likeness of God?"

Notes

1 Much of the material in this article is a condensed version of a three-part essay entitled "Human Dignity," originally appearing in the journal *Fu Jen International Religious Studies* 3.1 (Summer 2009), 1–58. I wish to thank the editors for permission to use this material.

2 Alexander Altmann, *"Homo Imago Dei* in Jewish and Christian Theology," *Journal of Religion* 48 (1968): 235–59.

3 Altmann, *"Homo Imago Dei,"* 259.

the Image and Likeness of God (Crestwood, NY: St. Vladimir's Seminary Press, 1974), especially chapter 6.

19 The most complete history of the development of notions of *contemplatio*, beginning with the Bible and Greek philosophers and continuing down through Christian history, is the multi-author article "Contemplation," in the *Dictionnaire de spiritualité*, 17 vols. (Paris: Beauchesne, 1937–94), Vol. 2, 1643–2193.

20 Thunberg, "Human Person," 306.

21 The problem of the role of corporality, especially in the Augustinian teaching on humanity, is discussed by M.-D. Chenu, "Situation Humaine: Corporalité et Temporalité," in *L'Homme et son destin d'après les penseurs du moyen âge* (Louvain/Paris: Nauwelaerts, 1960), 23–49.

22 For an overview of Christian understandings of the resurrection of the body, see Caroline Walker Bynum, *The Resurrection of the Body in Western Christianity, 200–1336* (New York: Columbia University Press, 1995), who treats Origen on pp. 63–71.

23 Maximus the Confessor, *Ambiguum* 7, as translated in *On the Cosmic Mystery of Jesus Christ. Selected Writings from St. Maximus the Confessor*, translated by Paul M. Blowers and Robert Louis Wilken (Crestwood, NY: St. Vladimir's Seminary Press, 2003), 66. For a summary of Maximus' teaching on the unity of human nature, see Thunberg, *Microcosm and Mediator*, 103–6.

24 On the evolution of the notion of microcosm, see Rudolf Allers, "Microcosmos from Anaximandros to Paracelsus," *Traditio* 2 (1944): 319–409.

25 *Difficulty (Ambiguum)* 41, as translated in Andrew Louth, *Maximus the Confessor* (London and New York: Routledge, 1996), 157.

26 Bernard of Clairvaux, *Sermones super Cantica Canticorum* 81.11.

27 Gregory of Nyssa, *De hominis opificio* 16–17.

28 See Willemien Otten, *The Anthropology of Johannes Scottus Eriugena* (Leiden: E.J. Brill, 1991).

29 A.C. Pegis, *At the Origins of the Thomistic Notion of Man* (New York: Macmillan, 1963), 58–59.

30 This "insofar as" (*inquantum*) principle, that is, speaking only of the formal quality and not of the concrete existence, is a key for understanding many of Eckhart's most daring statements. For an explanation, see Bernard McGinn, *The Mystical Thought of Meister Eckhart* (New York: Crossroad-Herder, 2001), 15–16, 89.

31 Meister Eckhart, Pr. 12.

32 Catherine of Siena, *Letter* T304, as found in *The Letters of Catherine of Siena*, translated by Suzanne Noffke, 4 vols. (Tempe: Arizona Center for Medieval and Renaissance Studies, 1988–2008), Vol. 3, 185.

3

'TOLLE, LEGE': *Reading and Discernment as a Source of Personal Transformation*

DAVID LONSDALE

CONTEXT AND QUESTIONS

In the Page-Barbour Lectures at the University of Virginia in 1933, which were later published as *After Strange Gods: A Primer of Modern Heresy*, T. S. Eliot lamented the lack of any strong tradition of ethical and religious, and specifically Christian, literary criticism, and made an eloquent plea for just such a practice to be established as a legitimate approach to the interpretation and criticism of works of literature which may or may not be themselves specifically and overtly religious.[1] This involves using a Christian theological and ethical framework as a means of analysing, interpreting and evaluating works of literature – poetry, novels, drama – and both in these lectures and in the later years of his life Eliot showed how he thought this should be done. He was criticized on at least two counts. For a person in his position to make such a public profession of Anglo-Catholicism was deeply unfashionable and many of his contemporaries simply could not see how a cultivated intellectual could be a Christian with any integrity. And he was accused of rejecting legitimate practices of literary criticism in favour of an approach driven by ideology and dogmatism, and an ideology and set of dogmas which

For many people the phrase 'the spiritual life' conjures up something still and luminous, turned to the future and far from our daily lives, where, spiritually, we just 'bump along'. I believe we can also speak of a 'received view' of spiritual life as involving long periods of quiet, focused reflection, dark churches, and dignified liturgies. In its higher reaches it involves time spent in contemplative prayer, retreats . . . Above all it involves solitude and collectedness. It does not involve looking after small children.[3]

Writers in all ages and in various cultures have noted and described the power of the book or of a written text, to change people for better or worse. A classic instance is the story of Paolo and Francesca in Dante's *Inferno*, Canto V, and many more examples could be given.[4] At the beginning of Canto V Dante and Virgil move on from the first to the second circle of Hell. After meeting Minos, they come to the place of the 'carnal sinners', where the light is dim and where a great, unending storm, with howling winds, carried the spirits hither and yon. After meeting the spirits of legendary lovers from the past, 'as one bewildered', Dante notices 'two that go together and seem so light upon the wind' (V, 73–75) and wants to speak to them. The two lovers are Paolo and Francesca; Francesca tells their story. One day Francesca and her brother-in-law, Paolo, were reading together the story of Lancelot and Guinevere. Francesca says, 'We were alone and without any misgiving' (V, 129). She goes on: 'Many times that reading drew our eyes together and changed the colour in our faces, but one point alone it was that mastered us; when we read that the longed-for smile was kissed by so great a lover, he who never shall be parted from me, all trembling, kissed my mouth.' (V, 130–36). They have been condemned to Hell, but Francesca seems to lay the blame for their plight upon the book and its author. 'A Galeotto [Galahad] was the book and he who wrote it; that day we read in it no farther' (V, 137–38). When Francesca ends her story, 'the other spirit wept', and Dante, who also wrote of love, 'for pity . . . swooned as if in death and fell like a dead body' (V, 142–43).

Here and in other examples a book or a text is seen to have a transforming influence, for good or ill, on the lives of readers (or listeners) transcendent 'existentials' of all human existence, one of its permanent characteristics:

> Human existence is inevitably and inescapably subject to certain transcendent conditions such that, while they may indeed be denied, they do not thereby cease to be so, and constantly remain in force whether we recognize them consciously or not, whether we accept them or protest against them.[8]

That is because each and every person is 'loved by God with the absolute and unreserved self-offering of the innermost depths of God's own true life'; because 'God has willed the incarnation of the eternal logos to take effect in his existence' and because 'the grace of God is applied to [each] permanently and enduringly'. The purpose of God's self-gift in love is 'to support the life of humanity from within'. Rahner understands grace in human life as an active force which 'appeals to all, empowers all and invites all'; 'it wells up from the depths of a person's heart in a thousand different ways'; it makes human beings restless, and it is through grace that human existence in all its aspects is constantly open to the infinite.[9]

Grace is also mediated through creation, history and the church: through sacraments, people, events, objects, activities, relationships, even those which are not overtly or in any obvious way religious or Christian.

In his reflections on writers and writing, Rahner argues that every act of writing, as a personal, moral act, represents a response, whether positive or negative, to grace. The act of writing, as the act of speaking, 'has a moral relevance prior to and independent of the content of what is being said', at least if it is considered in its formal aspect.[10] And this is true even though writers may not grasp the full significance of what they are saying or may be saying more than they intended. Consequently, according to Rahner, it would be wrong of Christians to dismiss the work of writers who are not explicitly Christian or who oppose Christianity. An author's expression of an 'anguished atheism' may in fact be in reality 'a sharing in the desolation of the Cross'.[11] And even when a writer implicitly or is speaking specifically about poetry, but his comments also apply to narrative. He quotes Borges, 'what is essential is . . . the thrill, the almost physical emotion that comes with each reading' and comments: 'Borges is talking about the fluid, exhilarating moment which lies at the heart of any memorable reading, the undisappointed joy of finding that everything holds up and answers the desire that it awakens'.[16] This moment of delight stems from the beauty of the poem, its being something 'fully realized',[17] the union of content and its play and patterns of sounds, its images, words, rhythms, what in the same lecture Heaney calls 'proportion and pace and measure', 'winding forms and woven metaphors'.[18] In both writing and reading, 'the movement is from delight to wisdom, and not vice versa'.[19]

READING AND DISCERNMENT

I would now like to consider some aspects of the experience of reading literary texts and the meeting between the world of the text and the world of the reader in the light of the Christian tradition of discernment of spirits. I begin by highlighting some parallels between reading literary texts and imaginative contemplation which is focused on biblical stories. That there are discernible affinities is not entirely surprising; after all imaginative contemplation is a form of *lectio divina*, 'holy reading'.

Both imaginative contemplation and reading poetry or a novel involve engaging with and entering into an imagined world, an alternative world, which is different from one's own. A few years ago I was talking to one of my nephews. He was about thirteen at the time. His dad had a complete set of Hornblower stories, and Dominic was about half way through the whole series and totally captivated. He said: 'Reading is brilliant. You can imagine the whole story for yourself, create your own pictures of the people, the scenes and the actions.' This is also what happens in imaginative contemplation and it forms the basic material for the kind of reflection on experience that we call discernment.

There are also, perhaps, some similarities between the predispositions desired of a reader on the one hand, and the person who engages in capacity to bring to light hidden parts of the landscape of the self, both good and bad, regions of grace and regions of sin. Likewise, studies of the process of reading literary texts also stress its capacity to bring about self-discovery, self-knowledge in the reader, to reveal what might so far have been hidden and to affirm or challenge ideas, values, assumptions, biases, hopes and aspirations which the reader has up to that point either been unaware of or has taken for granted. The reader interrogates the text and the text interrogates the reader.

It may be important to stress that 'loving attention' does not mean setting aside one's critical faculties or critical reflection. On the contrary, I would argue that critical reflection and evaluation are essential elements of loving attention. A critical awareness is essential to any realistic knowledge and love of others and of oneself. One of the lessons which deconstruction and feminist hermeneutics have taught us is the need for both generosity (loving attention) and 'suspicion' in reading, interpretation and evaluation. In imaginative contemplation and discernment based on it critical reflection is also vital. Here, however, it focuses not so much on the text (though critical-historical examination and even deconstruction of the text may also be an element in the contemplative process), but on the person who engages with the text and its impact in her world.

Moreover, in imaginative contemplation there is a movement from attention to the text itself and its world to the world of the person who is engaged in this activity. This movement is typically by way of such questions as: What does this mean for me? What are its implications for me, my values, my relationships, my choices, the shape and direction of my life, the person I am and the person I might be? This movement allows the experience of contemplation to have an impact on choices, actions, commitments, ways of living. Thus contemplation has practical consequences which are to a greater or lesser degree transformative. And this is the point at which discernment is a crucial element in the process, as a bridge between the experience of contemplation and the choices people make in everyday life. It has the capacity to help a person who engages in contemplation to explore the possible consequences of that activity in his or her life.

We might also reflect briefly on dispositions desirable in contemplation

I have already mentioned the experience of what Seamus Heaney calls 'delight'. Both imaginative contemplation and reading literature evoke in those who engage in them responses that the tradition thinks of as 'movements of the spirit'. Movements of desire, attraction and revulsion, joy and sorrow, delight and disappointment, confidence and fear, hope and desperation are aroused by engagement with the text. Traditionally, in contemplation, these movements are the focus of critical reflection as a guide to choices and action in life. In the next section of this discussion, I will set aside imaginative contemplation and focus on the position of readers of literary texts, and in particular the reader's transition from reading to evaluating and allowing what is read to have an impact on the reader's own choices and actions.

The Christian tradition of discernment as mediated by Ignatius Loyola, suggests two processes of rational reflection. The first is a reflection on the responses which reading has evoked in the reader. The second is a reflection on possible outcomes, the options, the choices which reading a literary text presents to the reader if the world of the text is to impinge in a practical way on the life and world of the reader. Both kinds of reflection are helpful and in practice they are two aspects of one activity of discernment. Both presuppose that a reader is not simply carried along by his responses to act on them impulsively, without reflection, and that readers, through reflection, can achieve some measure of 'distance' from their immediate responses.

Reflection on responses to literary texts

In this setting, the task of discernment is twofold: on the one hand, to discover where grace is present in readers' responses to texts and to help readers to make choices which are consonant with the direction is which grace is moving; on the other hand to spot the areas of resistance to grace and to explore ways of breaking down or overcoming that resistance.[26] The focus of attention is, therefore, not primarily the *content* of the text but the 'movements of the spirit' which arise in the reader in response to the text. With regard to these responses, three insights of Ignatius Loyola are particularly noteworthy.[27] The first insight is that consolation can appear to be authentic but may not be so in reality. A novel or a poem damaging to themselves and others. Grace works in both cases to foster the greater good and to stimulate and strengthen resistance to evil, but, crucially, through different kinds of experiences.

The purpose of discernment is to unmask illusion, to discriminate between the authentic and the deceptive or misleading in a person's dispositions and responses. The most important questions about a reader's responses to literary texts have to do not with their origin but with the *direction* in which these responses are leading: most especially whether they are leading towards a fuller human life for oneself and others or in the opposite direction. Important questions in a Christian context, therefore, might be: Does this work reinforce in me, the reader, a faith and trust that there is meaning and purpose in the world and in human life or does it strengthen a sense of meaninglessness and cynicism? Does it encourage hope or hopelessness? Is it leading through self-transcendence to a deepening and broadening of compassion and a desire for others' good or encouraging narcissism and self-absorption? Is it opening me to mystery? Is it faithful to the spirit of the Incarnation and the veneration of the sacred in the human? Is it consonant with the paschal mystery and the way of Christian discipleship? The answers to such questions as these are intended to help a reader make morally and spiritually discriminating choices in the light of reading literary texts.

Reflection on possible choices

The experience of reading and interpretation may suggest a range of options, forms of action 'inspired' by the text. As readers we need ways of discriminating between good and bad choices and Ignatius Loyola's guidance offers valuable forms of reflection and thought-experiments for this purpose. Here the material for reflection is not the reader's responses but the possible choices to which this reading might lead: what am I to do? What am I to be? The reflection consists in the well-known exercise of setting out and weighing the reasons for and against each of the options in the light of what the person faced with choices considers to be ultimate value and purpose.[29] This is a necessary move towards ensuring that choices are grounded in reality and based on those rational considerations and moral values which are significant for the person making which could be of use to teachers, chaplains and other mentors charged with helping the young to negotiate this phase of their lives.[31] Secondly, the same applies to those of us who are teaching or guiding students in mid-life, which is equally a time of disequilibrium, renegotiation of values and relationships and reordering of life. Thirdly, the conversation that I have been conducting between reading and Christian discernment may also offer something of value for those of us who are involved in spiritual direction of bookworms. Finally, this conversation raises questions for those of us who direct or supervise graduate and research students. Obviously they have to read fast (because they have to read so much in a short time), 'master' their texts and learn and practise sharp academic analysis of and critical reflection on the content of what they are studying. Those are skills that we, as teachers, want and need to foster. But in the light of the thoughts I have outlined here, I do wonder whether, as a supervisor, I might take more account of the kind of attention students pay to texts; whether there is something to be said for a more contemplative approach to texts alongside the essential skill of fast, analytic reading; and whether helping students to reflect more on their own responses to texts, along the lines that I have indicated, might also contribute something of value to their search for what is true and good and wise and to their growth as human beings.

Notes

1 T. S. Eliot, *After Strange Gods: A Primer of Modern Heresy* (London: Faber & Faber, 1934).
2 A recent book which outlines and offers a philosophical defence of such a practice is Luke Ferreter, *Towards a Christian Literary Theory* (Basingstoke, UK: Palgrave Macmillan, 2003).
3 Janet Martin Soskice, *The Kindness of God: Metaphor, Gender and Religious Language* (Oxford: Oxford University Press, 2007), pp. 12–13.
4 I have used the translation by John D. Sinclair, *The Divine Comedy of Dante Alighieri with Translation and Comment by John D. Sinclair* (New York: Oxford University Press, 1961). Other examples might include: the tale of King Yunan and Duban the doctor in *Tales from the Thousand and One Nights*; Augustine's *Confessions*, Book 9; Flaubert's *Madame Bovary*; *The*

4

'A transformative blending': Anthony de Mello (1931–87) on the Spiritual Exercises of St Ignatius Loyola

GERALD O'COLLINS, SJ

It has happened only twice in my life that I have become involved in editing some hitherto unpublished material. The first occasion came over thirty years ago when I published in 1974 some letters of an Irish-Australian statesman and politician, Patrick McMahon Glynn, who helped to write the Australian Constitution and from 1901 served for nearly twenty years as a member in the national parliament and a minister in three governments.[1] Now, with two Jesuit friends, Daniel Kendall and Jeffrey LaBelle, I have prepared for publication a much more important scoop: a course of transforming lectures that Anthony de Mello, SJ gave on the *Spiritual Exercises* of St Ignatius Loyola.[2]

For all those who cherish the legacy of Tony de Mello, this book will present and reveal something that has so far been missing in his published works: the well-spring of his own spiritual life. For de Mello, making the Spiritual Exercises for himself, directing those doing the Exercises, and teaching others to become skilled directors of the Exercises was the heart of the matter – his specifically Jesuit way to God. Let me first explain how this scoop came about.

times the language of Transactional Analysis.

Perhaps the most time-consuming part in editing this manuscript came when we verified and gave precise references to different authors, both past and present, when de Mello cited them. Here and there what he quoted by heart needed to be corrected. In the task of tracing some references, various friends – not least, Philip Endean, SJ – were of immense help.

Finally, Kendall, LaBelle and I had to trim Text C down to the length requirements of our New York publishers, Doubleday, and produce Text D. While we were sorry to drop some of de Mello's material, we found it a special blessing that our editor at Doubleday in New York was deeply committed to the project. He makes no secret of the fact that he owes to de Mello his faith in Jesus Christ. He has worked extremely hard on Text D to make the best of de Mello's thought on the *Exercises* accessible to a wider public through what he wants to become a genuine 'trade book'. For the sake of any specialists who want to do research on de Mello, we will deposit in the archives of the Californian Jesuit Province at Los Gatos the original copy we received from Albert Menezes (Text A), the transcript of that copy (Text B), and our original, fuller edition of de Mello's lectures (Text C). The published book (Text D) is entitled *Seek God Everywhere: Reflections on the Spiritual Exercises of St Ignatius* and is now widely available through bookstores and libraries.

When de Mello gave the talks that made up this book, he used (and sometimes criticized) the translation by Louis Puhl: *The Spiritual Exercises of St. Ignatius* (Chicago: Loyola University Press, 1951). Since de Mello taught his course in late 1975 and, in particular, since his untimely death in 1987, other translations have appeared: for instance, Joseph Munitiz and Philip Endean, *Saint Ignatius of Loyola: Personal Writings* (London: Penguin, 1996) and David Fleming, *Draw Me Into Your Friendship: A Literal Translation and Contemporary Reading of the Spiritual Exercises* (St Louis: Institute of Jesuit Sources, 1996). Many notable studies of the *Exercises* have also been published: for example, James Connor et al., *The Dynamism of Desire: Bernard J. F. Lonergan, S.J., on the Spiritual Exercises of Saint Ignatius of Loyola* (St Louis: Institute of Jesuit Sources, 2006); David Fleming (ed.), *Notes on the Spiritual Exercises of St Ignatius of Loyola* (St Louis: Review for Religious, 1981); and Michael in the proper proportions, you will produce results' (Introduction).

After proposing a prologue, the First Principle and Foundation, Ignatius divides the *Exercises* into four parts or 'weeks'. These 'weeks' can vary in length, and do not necessarily consist of seven days each. During the first week those making the Exercises meditate on sin and its consequences, with the aim of experiencing deep repentance or total turning to God. During the second week, the contemplations and meditations focus on the life of Jesus Christ. Ignatius includes during the second week: (1) an Introduction to the Consideration of Different States of Life; (2) a Meditation on the Two Standards (do the retreatants really want to serve under the standard of Christ and not under the standard of Satan?); (3) a Meditation on Three Classes of Persons (what are three, different ways for finding spiritual freedom and choosing what is best?); (4) a consideration of Three Kinds of Humility (how far will a person go in being entirely conformed to the will of Christ?).

The third week turns to contemplate Christ's passion and death, and in the fourth week those making the Exercises contemplate his resurrection and risen life. The final exercise is called 'The Contemplation for Attaining Love', the goal being to receive the grace of finding God in all things in a broader form of contemplation.

To help directors, Ignatius adds lengthy instructions or guidelines ('Annotations', as they were traditionally called); 'Additions' or additional directions; and various notes and rules – above all, the Rules for the Discernment of Spirits (Chapter 7).

The full course of Spiritual Exercises is made over a period of around thirty days. They can be adapted, abbreviated or lengthened, according to how much time people are free to devote to them, how fast each one makes progress, and so on. Ignatius held that the Exercises in their entirety should be made only once or twice in a person's lifetime.

In the more than 450 years since the *Spiritual Exercises* came into existence, innumerable people have made them and many authors have written about them. Every Jesuit is required to make them fully at least twice: at the beginning and at the end of his spiritual formation. As individual Jesuits come from and live in almost all parts of the world, their own context and culture affect the way they approach the *Spiritual* from? Who is pushing me? There is no substitute for this awareness, this coming home to oneself. See how superficial it is to say, "Forget yourself and lose yourself in others."' 'Self-awareness', he declares, 'is essential for love.'

This all leads de Mello to present Ignatius' examination of conscience as 'a very delightful exercise', which begins by praising and thanking God for the specific graces received during the day. 'People can say to themselves, "If I haven't received any graces today, then I was not at home." God sends deliveries constantly.' To establish contact with God, we must establish contact with ourselves. If people are strangers to themselves and not at home with themselves, how can they be close to God and to others?

For de Mello the examination of conscience can repeat questions from the first week of the *Exercises*: 'What have I done for Christ? What am I doing for Christ? What ought I to do for Christ?' To review a day under the loving gaze of Christ turns self-examination into a consoling, life-giving exercise.

(2) De Mello joins Ignatius in defining *retreat directors* as those who explain methods for meditating and contemplating. They show methods of prayer to retreatants and explain what they are to do. They should not give content for meditation. 'Unfortunately', he observes, 'over the years directors have degenerated into content-giving.'

De Mello has much to offer about ways of praying: for instance, on 'the application of the senses' or 'fantasy', as he calls it. It means sharing personally in the Gospel stories by 'living with Christ in fantasy, getting to know him that way, and falling in love with his way of life'. De Mello recognizes that some people object to this method and say: 'Christ is not actually being born today, not actually dying today. How can I imagine myself there?' De Mello responds by citing the saints and mystics who practised this method of prayer. St Anthony of Padua held in his arms the Child Jesus, even if he knew that Jesus was no longer an infant. St Teresa of Avila consoled Christ in his agony in the garden, even though she knew that he was

(3) Right from the outset de Mello highlights in his lectures the indispensable role of *silence and solitude* as conditions for spiritual growth. 'Silence', he assures his Sadhana group, 'is the greatest treasure we have.' Silence can be 'painful', but it brings 'purification' and allows us to confront ourselves and God. Through silence we 'come in touch' with God. 'In that sense, everything is found in silence' (Introduction). The refreshing sweetness of silence is necessary not only for prayer but also for full human living. 'There is only one way for people to confront themselves and that is through silence, by developing a tolerance for silence, a home to themselves, a place to touch the well-springs of life inside themselves.'

De Mello stresses the need, and sometimes pain, of getting in touch with ourselves through silence. 'One of the biggest escapes during a retreat', he adds, 'is spiritual reading. That way people run away from the pain of confronting themselves and God . . . People need to face the pain of silence.' People take up books and read 'in the way a husband reads his newspaper during breakfast, so that he will not need to talk to his wife. Reading is a nice defence. Such people are reading all about God, but are not exposing themselves to him.'

To illustrate what he wants to say about silence, he draws on a variety of authors, old and new: from Thomas Merton to Simone Weil, and from desert fathers to Evelyn Underhill. But, as often happens in de Mello's lectures, the most vivid paragraphs come when he turns very personal and recalls experiences of silence and its effects. 'We must always be silent', he concludes, 'to pick up a flash of the infinite, of the eternal.'

(4) The experience of silence is indispensable for coming to terms with *inordinate attachments* or 'vested interests' that influence our thinking and praying. Self-deception is pervasive and leads people to put a whole wall of reasons around the things they want to defend. Ignatius does not argue with such people but gets at them in the only way he can, a deeply effective way. He makes such persons 'fall in love with Christ, and so mysteriously and "irrationally" fall in love with the

Borgia: 'Knowing within ourselves that without these consolations all our thoughts, words and actions are tainted, cold and disordered, we ask for them, so that with them we may become pure, warm and upright.' In other words, the situation is good only insofar as it is flooded with consolation. 'So ask for it', de Mello insists.

Using the image of a sailboat, De Mello puts Ignatius' attitude this way: 'we have got consolation. Surrender to it. Give in to it completely, because we will travel miles and miles; go right ahead. Then the wind drops. What should you do? Pick up your oars? No, start asking for the consolation to come back.' We need, of course, to examine ourselves: 'Where did I go wrong?' 'Change what went wrong', de Mello proposes. 'Consolation will soon return. Wait for the wind; it will come back. It is only in consolation that we really make progress in true and solid spiritual virtues.'

To clinch his point, de Mello quotes from someone often considered to be the spiritual successor of Mahatma Gandhi, Vinoba Bhave (1895–1982): 'Have you noticed how you keep dragging a boat along the sand? It's so heavy; fifty men can hardly pull it; and then the tide comes in, and two children can pull that boat.' This, de Mello observes, is 'what happens when God's grace floods into our hearts. Everything becomes so easy.'

(6) After citing de Mello on self-awareness, the role of directors in teaching methods and prayer, the essential place of silence not only for retreats but also for prayer, dealing with inordinate attachments, and the indispensable role of consolation for spiritual progress, I want to round off this sample of 'precious themes' by summarizing what he proposes (in Chapter 1) on one exercise, the first principle and foundation. He understands what can seem a spare, dry and very logical text to express what it is to move beyond merely relative reality and fall in love with the Absolute – something that can give us only serenity and peace. The 'secret of human life', he insists, is to get in touch with the Absolute and achieve 'union with the Absolute'. Then everything else will make sense and fall into place.

Here de Mello presses into service what Blessed Charles de

(2) De Mello understands the fruit of the first week of the *Exercises* to be an 'intense desire for God', which will be 'the foundation of everything else' (Chapter 3). Here de Mello introduces the kind of Indian illustration that readers have cherished in his well-known books:

> A man goes to a sadhu [Hindu ascetic] every day and says he wants to experience God. The sadhu gives no reply, and the man comes back again and again and again. After many days the sadhu says: "This man seems to be an earnest seeker of God." So, he tells him: "When I go down for a bath in the river, come and meet me there." They both enter the water, and the sadhu pushes the man's head under the water for a minute or two. He is struggling to get out. The sadhu releases him and says: "When I held your head under the water, you were struggling to get out. Why?" "Because I was gasping for air," the man replies. The sadhu tells him: "The day you desire God so earnestly as you desired air when you were under the water, that day you will find him."

(3) In discussing the Three Degrees of Humility, de Mello expounds Ignatius' remark about not 'giving cause' for humiliations and refers to St Teresa of Avila and Joseph Rickaby, SJ (1845–1932). A novice once went to see Teresa 'and asked if she would say stupid things at recreation so that she would be humiliated. Teresa replied: "More stupid things?" And the novice was very hurt!' Rickaby once wrote: 'Don't make an attempt to make a fool of yourself, but be resigned when you are found out.' 'So', de Mello adds, 'Ignatius tells us not to give cause for being humiliated, but when we're "found out" to rejoice. Here he inculcates the liberation of the total person. So long as we do not have these dispositions, we will never be in lasting peace.'

(4) On dying to oneself, de Mello mentions a monk from Taizé who put the solution this way: 'Sometimes I had left Christ for my neighbour, and sometimes I had left my neighbour for Christ. One

(1) The first appendix ('Why Make a Retreat?') includes four loosely connected items. In one of his talks de Mello presented 'entering and making a retreat'; the Benedictine method of prayer; the First Principle and Foundation, to which he had already dedicated a talk (= chapter 1 in Text D); and some further aspects of the First Week of the *Exercises*.

(2) The second appendix, 'Quieting the Mind', comes from a talk on contacting God through meditation that draws on a variety of classical authors: Abbot John Chapman, (anonymous) *The Cloud of Unknowing* (one of de Mello's favourite books), St John of the Cross, St Teresa of Avila, and other classical authors. The challenge is to quieten the mind while developing the 'faculty through which we receive an intuition of the infinite Being'. It is the faculty (called variously 'heart', 'high mind', 'will') for 'grasping God without concepts, images, thoughts, or words'. The mystics say that this faculty 'cannot be developed; it is given by God. Most of all, they advise us to do nothing. When the mind cannot focus any more in prayer, then wait and rest until God comes and gives us this other faculty.'

(3) 'The Jesus Prayer', to which de Mello himself used to dedicate a whole conference during retreats, forms the content of our third appendix. It was one of the ways he would teach people *how* to pray. He linked the Jesus Prayer (as described in *The Way of a Pilgrim*) to the use of mantras in Sanskrit and other languages (including Latin).

(4) The fourth and final appendix may be the shortest, but seems the most powerful. It comes from a talk on 'death fantasies'. De Mello proposes for prayer four of these fantasies, the last being attending in imagination one's own funeral. These four fantasies concerned with death and the approach of death may be somewhat frightening, but they put things into perspective, could help to heal memories, and would provide a powerful incentive to settle unfinished business.[4]

At the start I called the chance of editing these lectures on the *Exercises*

5

Visionary Women: From Past Icons to Future Inspiration

BERNADETTE FLANAGAN

In choosing a title for this chapter, I chose the phrase 'visionary women' without too much questioning or doubt. The concept sprang from that unconscious reservoir of formative literature which grows and expands in each of us over the course of our lives as scholars. At times I sense that research generates in the researcher an intuitive cataloguing system. This system ensures that concepts which we have encountered earlier in our research lives, that will be of assistance in later work, remain readily accessible. This process creates a discernible genealogy of influences which can be mapped between our later work and our earlier work.

In my genealogical chart, I attach particular significance to Elizabeth Petroff's 1986 edited publication *Medieval Women's Visionary Literature*,[1] which I first read in 1991. In her Introduction to the collection of writings from medieval visionary women she had assembled, Petroff reflected on the significance of the 'visionary' genre. For Petroff it is essentially a time-conditioned mode of autobiography. As those who explore the narrative self in autobiography today can identify trends in the casting of characters, in the unfolding of desire and its transformation and in the contours of plot as emergent design, so Petroff sets out the seven genres of self-narrative which visionary literature presents. Following Petroff's lead I wish to turn to a thematically organized collection of women's literature, and explore in this literature impulses towards transformation and so it was necessary to bring the film back for a second run – the only film in the 2007 listings to require a second screening. This 162-minute documentary created an experience for the viewer of the intense solitude of Carthusian life in the nine-hundred-year-old Grand Chartreuse monastery. A similarly unexpected positive reception of this award-winning documentary was experienced in Germany and Italy. The film maker, Philip Gröning, in an interview regarding the film views it as not merely documentary but rather didactic: 'the time when you can base your self-concept on work is over . . . and everyone is afraid of what will happen next. . . . The function of a human being is not to work. The function of a human being is to be aware'.[6]

A changing sense of the meaning of some of the core practices of monastic life has presented itself to me not only in cinema, but also in the classroom. For almost ten years, in the late nineties and into the new millennium, I taught in Milltown Institute, Dublin, a module entitled, *Consecrated Life: Theology and Practice*. Each year, the same sessions in the module seemed to have an engaging and enlivening effect on the participants. The sessions in question were the ones where the history of consecrated life was presented. An important text for this presentation was Philip Sheldrake's article, 'Revising Historical Perspectives', which was published in an edition of *The Way Supplement* that explored the theme 'Religious Life in Transition'.[7] In this article Sheldrake challenged the reader to 'question the assumption, not only that the foundational model for religious life was cenobitic-monastic, but that its development moved in a single line'.[8] He went on to outline the many expressions of the committed, singular quest for God which are regularly excluded from an account of the history of consecrated life. These expressions, particularly the Beguines, always generated imaginative engagement for participants in the module and most significantly among the women students. It is in the spirit of thoughtful seeking for transformed expression of intentional spiritual questing which came to attention during these discussions that I approach my current project.

New rich interpretations of the practices associated with the God quest – responsible stewardship, fasting, pilgrimage, solitude, social solidarity and asceticism – are re-configuring the discussion of religious the current emergence of intentional solitude-embracing spiritual living by women today. The choice of lives which I have made is meant to be suggestive rather than comprehensive, but patterns will emerge which might not otherwise be observed.

I am proposing that the reflections of women who have lived or now live spiritually committed lives which embrace forms of intentional solitude or silence can enrich the living understanding of new monasticisms. My goal is to set out a research trail which others can return to and fill in more comprehensively. I shall draw attention to coincidences between past and present, between theoretical frameworks and social realities, which when assembled together present a picture that is not revealed by considering the parts separately.

MONINNE/DARERCA (C. 432–518)[13]

There is in Ireland a hidden history of women forging singular paths of spiritual innovation. Research has shown, for example, how in an early life of Brigit of Kildare a story is told about a religious woman who lived on her own and did not have adequate resources to create a meal of welcome for a visit of Brigit that would do justice to Brigit's social stature. When this story from her life was being redacted in a twelfth-century account of Brigit's life the woman receiving Brigit is no longer presented on her own, but as living in a small group of women.[14] In a similar way, we find that while primary Irish women saints are noted by name and individually for their religious innovation, there tends to be a focus on the later phases of their lives when surrounded by companions, rather than the earlier solitary stage as religious innovators.[15]

The architectural structure of early monastic communities in Ireland is notable for the space provided for an individual's spiritual journey within a communal Gospel journey. Small dwelling spaces were dispersed in groups throughout a large common shared space. The solitude which such a single dwelling space provided was unknown outside monastic enclosures since 'it was colder and more dangerous and a waste of precious space and fuel'.[16] Small communal prayer spaces – oratories – were 'she made great progress in a short time'.[21] Local opportunities for more advanced study were limited and so later she moved to the west coast of Ireland with some companions to be mentored by Bishop Ibar of the Aran Islands,[22] a man who also appears in the life of Brigit of Kildare as a supportive mentor.

After some time Ibar left the Aran Islands to travel to Wexford in the south-east of Ireland. Moninne and her companions travelled with him. En route they separated and Moninne spent time with Brigit in Kildare in the centre of Ireland. The accounts of her life tell us that for her companions Moninne was 'second only to Brigit in holiness of life, honesty of character and grace of virtues'.[23] Many fruitful encounters between two similarly inspired women are evoked by this conjoined reference of Moninne and Brigit. Moninne's choice to spend time with Brigit probably reflects the need for those who wish to move out the frontiers of emerging religious consciousness to engage in creative conversations with other visionary companions.

Moninne was empowered by her conversations with Brigit to give a first expression to her own personal calling and so she left Kildare to re-join Ibar who in the meantime had become established in Beggary Island in Wexford. This time, however, she joined him as a teacher. Ibar could provide the support of the skilled mentor during her first efforts to creatively express her personal vocation. Again, in this setting her profound capacity to connect with the longings, hopes and aspirations of the people of her time and country is evident in the crowds that she draws: 'not only women but also men desired to join the holy nun; even if they were endowed with ample dignity, they held it to be a great thing if they deserved to receive the blessing of the very holy nun'.[24]

Her inspirational life did not only consist in a private holiness; it also expressed itself in a deep compassion for those who were poor. The strength of this commitment was occasionally even a point of tension and there were complaints about the balance she exercised in the way she used communal resources since it sometimes seemed to excessively favour the poor visitor over her regular Beggary Island dwellers.[25] This reaction to the unfolding external expression of her inner spiritual insight reflects what is often a characteristic experience in the first stage of creative occasions she is entertained by guests and in return creates a rich supply of wine or ale[28] which endures even after her departure.

Thus, her relentless active solicitude for her own people, especially those who were poor or ill, is balanced in the biography with accounts of her immersion in desert space. The biographer refers to her as 'the daughter of John the Baptist and the prophet Elias'. This description is eremitically evocative, because in Matthew's Gospel (3.1-3) John's life is set 'in the wilderness of Judea' while Elias (Elijah) was a man of the tribe Aaron who was fed by ravens from God in the Wadi Cherith (1 Kings 17).

Moninne's times of solitude were spent 'in prayer and vigils' and in general 'follow(ed) in the footsteps of the earlier hermits'.[29] She follows the universal journey of insightful religious innovators in this withdrawal to solitary space, which enables freedom to be maintained through nurtured attentive awareness. Entering the 'desert' space represents the distance she puts between herself and the established culture and life forms of her society. While there is much to learn from her daily engagements, it is in the silence that the learnings are harvested, tasted and digested. In the practice of removing herself from the busyness of her daily life she is seeking to embrace the wisdom which creative indifference can yield.

The reception of the religious innovation being inaugurated through the movement she leads is, however, conditioned by the consciousness of the times in which she lived. Her biographer therefore bestows the ultimate accolade on her spiritual genius by declaring that 'she had a man's soul in a woman's body'.[30] The pervasive paradigm of the female person was that it was not holy, but rather a frail and unreliable species. Gillian Cloke's extensive research on this subject concludes:

anyone holy enough to be an exemplar of the faith could not *be* a woman: every one of the many who achieved fame through piety was held to 'surpass her sex' – never, be it noted, to elevate the expectations that might be held of her sex. The argument is self-fulfilling: however many of this kind of women there were, in being superior they were always exceptional from their sex, never taken to Killevy would enable future leaders to continuously renew so as to improve the service of the community in which they were embedded, detach from undesirable developments, and respond creatively to the unexpected.

One final incident which occurs close to the end of Moninne's life illustrates the central dynamic which was the root and sap of her flourishing foundation. Moninne shares her intuitive sense with her companions that there is a concealment of a compromising choice which a member of the group has made. She has no desire to use her leadership role to elicit the truth through fear-based injunctions. Instead, she enables the group to realize that together they create sustaining intimacy within their common life. In the empathic atmosphere which she creates in the group the withholding member comes forward to acknowledge that she received a gift from a man with whom she had an illicit affair.[34] Moninne's invitation to some group members to assist their companion in bringing her life into unity around her core commitment (through a ritual of supporting her in disposing of the gift) and her conclusion of the incident in a thanksgiving celebration all display profound insight into strategies for creating life-giving, sustainable spiritually supportive networks.

In the account of Moninne's life that I have given I am suggesting ways of reading which resist a dried-paint representation of women and which enable Moninne to be a teacher to women who are taking up similar journeys today. In the longer version of the project from which this material is extracted many more women will be placed in the unbroken line of singular women religious innovators, but within the confines of this chapter, I want to move on to a contemporary emerging literature which reflects the transmutation of the Moninne life-commitment into a contemporary form.

CONTEMPORARY SOLITUDE WRITERS

All over the world at this time new modes of weaving practices of intentional solitude and compassion into the fabric of life are emerging. Karen Karper Fredette and Paul Fredette, who live in North Carolina, have over

Later in her memoir she clarifies further the purpose of honouring solitude in her life:

As a hermit, I seek solitude, not so much to be alone as to bring together in myself all the disparate strands of life in our world. It is not a work I can do; only the Spirit can accomplish this re-weaving into unity; I am privileged to be part of the loom.

CECILIA WILMS

As well as Karper Fredette's own experience being of assistance in mapping the new solitude movement that is happening, the *Raven's Bread* newsletter has also been very useful in providing narrative accounts of women in a great variety of circumstances who are undertaking the journey into solitude today. A typical example is an obituary on 13 May 1998 in *Raven's Bread* on the death of Cecilia Wilms, a hermit of Our Lady of the City Hermitage in Spokane, Washington.[39] Cecilia had been born in 1932 in Ghent, Belgium, and at age twenty-one joined the Cistercian Abbey of Our Lady of Nazareth at Brecht, which has historical associations with the thirteenth-century mystic Beatrijs van Nazareth (1220–68). When this monastery made the foundation of Redwoods Monastery in California in 1962, Cecilia moved to the United States. Four years later she took a leave of absence and began a new phase in her journey of monastic living. She lived in a poor neighbourhood of Spokane close to Gonzaga University, Washington, where she was employed part-time. Her interpretation of the journey she was travelling is available in the articles and excerpts from her journal which she published in *Contemplative Review* and other publications. As the following poem shows, her writings offer a rich sense of the deeply personal call which is being enacted by new monastics following a call into unmapped territory of new practices of silence or solitude:

I am a woman . . .
Called by the Lord

Embracing the Solitary Life (1999).[43] The former is quite eloquent in its description of learning the language of silence:

> In my possessive stalking of silence, I had sought to capture it, rip-ping it from its source of holiness. But it refused to be entombed by me, it withdrew so completely I had no way to follow it. When I gave up hope, *then* it illumined itself . . . *Open your heart*, it seemed to say, *and wait without waiting.*[44]

In diligently following the journey to which she was drawn Taylor gradually identified core practices which gave shape and structure to her commitment. Her second book provides a description of these practices – silence, solitude, simplicity, solidarity, obedience and prayer. For her the integrated living of these practices deepens human authenticity. As she notes, 'those who deliberately choose solitude are not posturing as holy people. They are simply trying to recapture true humanity in an increas-ingly image-driven world'.[45] For Taylor silence is the royal road to the utter poverty of the human condition and so leads to the point of utter communion with humanity. This discovery resonates for her[46] with some of the teaching in John of the Cross's the 'Spiritual Canticle':

> She lived in solitude,
> And now in solitude has built her nest
> And now in solitude he guides her
> He alone, Who also bears
> In solitude the wound of love.[47]

Karen Karper Fredette, Cecilia Wilms and Barbara Erakko Taylor are just the first three entries in a story of the new transformed expression of women's eternally alert spiritual sensibility. Many others' narratives will be added to the list over time,[48] such as Sara Maitland's explora-tion of the stages of the journey into solitude in *A Book of Silence*[49] or Sue Halpern's discussion of the diversity of forms solitude, chosen and un-chosen, in *Migrations to Solitude*[50] or Annemarie Kidder's portrayal of lived solitude through the centuries and its new manifestations today

Online, 11/3 (1996). Online: http://www.socresonline.org.uk/11/3/mac varish.html (accessed 11 August 2008).

3 See http://www.medusanet.ca/singlewomen/index.htm (accessed 11 August 2008).

4 'A woman religious living outside of cloister is . . . like a tree that is not rooted in the earth; . . . or a fish that is out of water . . . or a sheep that is not in its sheepfold and is in danger of being devoured by wolves' (my translation).

5 A German film maker, Philip Gröning, applied in 1984 to the Grand Chartreuse to film the Carthusian way of life. Sixteen years later the community was ready to receive him as a guest for six months, during which time he made the film without the usual technical supports that film makers use. The film won a Special Jury Prize at the Sundance festival in 2006.

6 See *Journal of Religion and Film* 10/1 (2006). Online: http://www.unomaha. edu/jrf/vol10no1/sundance2006.htm (accessed 15 August 2008).

7 P. Sheldrake, 'Revising Historical Perspectives', *The Way Supplement* 65 (1989): 66–77.

8 Sheldrake, 'Revising Historical Perspectives', 68.

9 M. Foucault, *The History of Sexuality: Volume Two: The Use of Pleasure* (New York: Vintage Books, 1990), 10–11.

10 S. Elm, '*Virgins of God': The Making of Asceticism in Late Antiquity* (Oxford: Clarendon Press, 1994).

11 B. Lane, *The Solace of Fierce Landscapes: Exploring Desert and Mountain Spirituality* (Oxford: Oxford University Press, 1998).

12 See S. Schneiders, *The Revelatory Text: Interpreting the New Testament as Sacred Scripture* (Collegeville, MN: Liturgical Press, 1999) and E. Schüssler Fiorenza, *Bread Not Stone: The Challenge of Feminist Biblical Interpretation* (Boston: Beacon Press, 1995).

13 The available lives of Moninne/Monenna/Moninna date from the eleventh or early twelfth century. Earlier texts are presumed to be the source of the available lives. See R. Sharpe, *Medieval Irish Saints' Lives: An Introduction to Vitae Sanctorum Hiberniae* (Oxford: Oxford University Press, 1991), 396–97. It has to be acknowledged that the lives of women from the early Irish Christian era are primarily communicated in a hagiographical genre. Recent research into this genre of writing has changed the reception of lives wrapped in this narrative tradition. It is no longer considered to be simply a devotional genre, amplifying the holiness of the saint; rather hagiography is now considered to offer a window on the society which produced it (M. Herbert, 'Hagiography', in K. McCone and K. Simms [eds], *Progress in Medieval Irish Studies* [Maynooth: St Patrick's College, 1996], 79–90). Against this background, University College Dublin scholar Elva Johnston has argued that 'Irish hagiography bears the imprint of an

17 M. and L. de Paor, *Early Christian Ireland* (London: Thames & Hudson, 1958), 54.

18 Bitel, *Isle of the Saints*, 63.

19 L. Bitel, 'Women's Monastic Enclosures in Early Ireland: A Study of Female Spirituality and Male Monastic Mentalities', *Journal of Medieval History* 12 (1986): 15–36.

20 Sperber, *The Life*, 74.

21 Sperber, *The Life*, 69.

22 The motif of women religious innovators being educated by male mentors is quite common in lives from this era. See C. Harrington, *Women in a Celtic Church: Ireland 450–1150* (Oxford: Oxford University Press, 2002), 232ff.

23 Sperber, *The Life*, 69.

24 Sperber, *The Life*, 70.

25 Sperber, *The Life*, 69–70.

26 According to Helen Noyes Webster, who interpreted the use of garlic on a journey in her book *Herbs, How to Grow Them and How to Use Them* (Boston: Branford, 1947), the Israelites travelling with Moses missed the garlic they had in Egypt when they went towards the Promised Land because if Moses had carried garlic, the Israelites may have been able to avoid intestinal putrefaction from eating the desert's available lizards and snakes: 'We remember the fish we used to eat in Egypt for nothing, the cucumbers, the melons, the leeks, the onions, and the *garlic*' (Num. 11.5).

27 Sperber, *The Life*, 71. In many cultures garlic is perceived as providing protection against spirits.

28 Sperber, *The Life*, 72, 73.

29 Sperber, *The Life*, 74.

30 Sperber, *The Life*, 74.

31 G. Cloke, *This Female Man of God: Women and Spiritual Power in the Patristic Age, AD 350–450* (London: Routledge, 1995), 220.

32 Callan, 'St Darerca and her Sister Scholars', 32.

33 Sperber, *The Life*, 75–76. For a discussion of whether the location of this monastery is in Galloway, Wales or Cornwall, see C. Thomas, '*Rosnat, Rostat*, and the early Irish Church', *Ériu* 22 (1971): 100–6.

34 Sperber, *The Life*, 76.

35 P. Fredette and K. Karper Fredette, *Consider the Ravens: On Contemporary Hermit Life* (New York: iUniverse, 2008).

36 Fredette and Karper Fredette, *Consider the Ravens*, 58–67.

37 K. Karper, *Where God Begins to Be: A Woman's Journey into Solitude* (New York: iUniverse, 1994).

38 Ibid., 18.

39 J. Weaver, 'An American Desert Mother', *Raven's Bread* 2/3 (1998): 3–4.

PART TWO

*Spiritual Classics and
Contemporary Experience*

6

Spiritual Transformation in *Augustine's* On the Trinity

EDWARD HOWELLS

Augustine's *On the Trinity* is widely discussed as a doctrinal work, for instance on the questions of the unity, consubstantiality and equality of the divine Persons, but much less as a work of spirituality.[1] Yet on reading the work as a whole, it is clear that alongside these doctrinal questions, *On the Trinity* describes a journey of faith, moving from the sending of the Son and Holy Spirit to our transformation into the life of the Trinity, which culminates in the 'face to face' knowing of heaven that Paul speaks of in 1 Corinthians 13, when 'I shall know even as I am known'.[2] I shall argue that *On the Trinity* is centrally concerned with spiritual transformation, and specifically with the trinitarian nature of contemplation. To interpret it in this way, I shall treat love as the central theme of the work, around which the other themes that I would like to consider, of relationality, transformation and knowing, are brought together.

A significant objection to the view that *On the Trinity* is concerned with spiritual transformation towards the goal of contemplation is to be found in the frequent comments that Augustine makes about the difference between the kind of knowing described in his famous mental trinities – where he likens the Trinity to the internal structure of the mind – and the nature of the Trinity itself. He may be quoted as saying, repeatedly, that we still do not know the Trinity as it is in God (VII, 11; XV, 23–26, 43); that we cannot yet fix on the face to face contemplation incarnation. Christ's humility – his birth of a woman and abuse at the hands of men, culminating in an unjust death – draws us to God in love, and our love in return is characterized by humility modelled on Christ, so that we are purified of competitive, possessive mental habits and transformed into the pattern of receiving power from another rather than taking pleasure in our own power (VIII, 7, 11; I, 3; IV, 2; XII, 14–15; XIII, 12, 17–18, 22–23). This is to receive the Holy Spirit poured out in our hearts, which transforms us into a relationship with God like the relationality of the Holy Spirit in the Trinity, where, as Augustine says, there are no 'ownership rights' among the givers (*dominatio dantium*; XV, 36, p. 424), but pure giving with nothing held back, in mutual surrender.

The feature of this transformed relationality on which Augustine focuses is that unity and distinction between the partners are simultaneous and within the same act. He finds this kind of relationality first in the Trinity. As Rowan Williams has said, to understand the divine nature as relational is 'the central element in Augustine's analysis' in *On the Trinity* as a whole.[4] The three Persons are distinct by virtue of their relationality, rather than as separate substances, and together they are one substance (V, 6, 12, 15). A good illustration of this point comes in Augustine's example of the bond between friends. Imagine, he says, that we could think of two men who are friends solely in respect of their friendship, and not by seeing them as two men substantially, who can be separated and can cease to be friends. If they were purely friends and not separable as men, they would exist only relatively to each other, which is like the Trinity (IX, 5–6). The same kind of relationality exists between us and God in the charity given by the Holy Spirit. In charity, two are united in such a way that their unity is the same as their distinction. Augustine says that there are three in charity: the lover, the beloved, and love itself (VI, 7; VIII, 14). The bond of love between the lover and the beloved contains both their unity and their distinction. This understanding of the nature of our relationship with God, derived directly from reflection on the doctrine of the Trinity, is the subject of Augustine's mental trinities, in the second half of *On the Trinity*. He turns to the image of God within the human mind in order to explore how we can be joined to God with the relationality of the Holy Spirit. In particular, he wants to consider our neighbour, for instance, we can be aware of the source of that love within ourselves. Furthermore, we can also see inwardly that this love has its source in love itself, which Augustine identifies with God. Therefore, jumping ahead in his argument, he says that we can know God's presence within our love for our neighbour, as the source of love's binding power in relation to others (VIII, 12). The task of becoming aware of God for Augustine, in such a way that we do not turn God into a false external object, is to examine the deep source of love within us and expand our awareness of it.

In Books IX and X, Augustine can be seen as developing tools towards this end, which help us recognize the presence of love within ourselves (IX, 2).[5] He regards our ability to 'see love' as rooted in the way that we know ourselves. He understands self-knowledge here not as a self-absorbed act of introspection, but as our inner awareness when engaged in love, which is directed outwards, both to God and to our fellow creatures. We look inward not to know ourselves apart from others but to examine how we are deeply *with* others, and supremely with God. In our inner love, he says, we find the same pattern as in the charity of the Holy Spirit, where the lover is united to the beloved in the bond of love at the same time as being distinguished from them. In Book IX, he focuses on how we can *know* this love, in our self-knowledge. When the mind seeks to know something, he says, it goes out in a kind of love to join with the object that it seeks to know, and at the same time is able to judge what it knows apart from the object. Thus, inwardly, the mind is able to both unite with and differentiate what it knows, at once. Augustine identifies this as the moment that we produce what he calls an 'inner word', before anything is expressed outwardly (IX, 13–16). We can understand this as a kind of 'approval' that the mind makes of itself, at the origin of knowing (IX, 16). In self-knowing, we can see it most clearly, because the mind is both loving and distinguishing *itself*, at once. Without developing Augustine's thought on this complex point more fully, the point to note is that the mind is structured by love, and knows by means of love. Its deepest act of knowing is to differentiate its own relational activity. We therefore possess an ability to see love at the source of our own relationality, in our inner awareness.

to differentiate God's relationality with us from within. We then possess our knowledge of God in an act of relationship which is the same as God's relationship with us.[7] We can be said to have not just knowledge *of* God, but a knowing immediately shared with God, sharing in the same act of relationship by which God first relates to God, as the Holy Spirit. This is contemplation. There is a journey of faith to be undergone, to repair and expand our capacity to see charity into the face to face vision of God. We will not be able to 'fix' our gaze on God in this way until heaven (XV, 50), although we can (and must) begin this journey here. Augustine is clear that our love and knowledge are not exactly the same as the inner life of the Trinity, because our mental hardware is not the same as the Trinity (XV, 22–26). Nevertheless, the structure of relationality in the human mind is precisely that of the charity given by the Holy Spirit, so that we can truly *share* our loving and knowing with God, and know God as a differentiation internal to this relationship, rather than externally. This is the goal of transformation in *On the Trinity*.

CONCLUSION

There are further ways in which our ability to 'see charity' is developed by Augustine in *On the Trinity*, which there is not space to consider here.[8] But we have seen enough to recognize that the work as a whole is directed to our spiritual transformation. We are created in the image of God, which Augustine works out in terms of our capacity to differentiate charity from within, at the roots of our knowing, in a manner modelled on the relationality of the Trinity. We need the external revelation of the incarnation and the sending of the Holy Spirit to turn us away from the pride and possessiveness of the fallen mind, so that we are receptive to the shared nature of charity, but once within this relationality, we find that we have the ability to know it inwardly, in the structure of our created minds. The mental trinities on which Augustine focuses are best read as tools which help us to discern the presence of God within us, when we turn to God in faith. They are intended to show us that we can know God in the very same act of relationship by which God knows us. Rowan which truly relates the Trinity as it is in God to our human lives, towards the goal of contemplation.

2 A page and a half of references to this verse are given in the CCSL edition of *De Trinitate* (CCSL L, *Aurelii Augustini Opera* Pars XVI, 2 Vols),Vol. 2, pp. 690–91.

3 In speaking of love as the central theme in *On the Trinity*, I am bringing out the 'volitional' and 'interpersonal' aspects of Augustine's treatment of the *imago dei*, more than the 'intellectual' aspect – to pick up on the three categories or 'traditions' of *imago dei* theology outlined by Bernard McGinn in his chapter in this volume (see p. 23 above and McGinn's Endnote 11). This is in part to balance over-intellectualist accounts of Augustine.

4 Rowan Williams, '*Sapientia* and the Trinity: Reflections on the *De Trinitate*', 332.

5 I am interpreting Augustine's two mental trinities, introduced in Books IX and X, as following directly from the inner trinity of love in Book VIII, and as expanding the trinity of love, rather than (as a number of commentators have suggested) treating them as a new departure which is necessary because the trinity of love fails in Augustine's argument.

6 Augustine's further reflections on the role of memory in Book XIV expand on this possibility, but there is not space in this short chapter to set this out.

7 This is a similar relationship to the one quoted by Bernard McGinn in his chapter in this volume, from Meister Eckhart, where Eckhart says, 'the eye with which I see God is the same eye with which God sees me', though Eckhart goes further than Augustine in his expression of the identity between God and the soul here (see p. 31 above and McGinn's Endnote 31).

8 In particular, the sense in which Augustine regards this loving seeing as *unknown*, in the respect that it is not merely possessed for ourselves but shared with others, and supremely with God, thus extending beyond what we can grasp for ourselves alone, is vital to his understanding.

7

Augustinian Anxiety and the Creation of Narrative in William of St Thierry

JEREMY WORTHEN

Wolfgang Iser, discussing *The Pilgrim's Progress* in an influential work of modern literary criticism, emphasizes the importance of the doctrine of predestination – as a doctrine in whose perpetual shadow the Puritans lived – in shaping Bunyan's fiction. According to Iser, *Pilgrim's Progress* 'filled a psychic gap that had been created by the doctrine of predestination'.[1] In this chapter, I will argue that William of St Thierry's creation of narrative in the *Meditativae orationes* five centuries earlier also has something to do with the energy of anxiety generated by Augustinian theology.[2] In order to do this, I need to begin by questioning the autobiographical interpretation of William's text that has often been taken for granted, before sketching out its narrative framework and relating that to Augustinian themes of grace and predestination. Finally, I shall come back to the issue of possible parallels with the seventeenth-century situation Iser is describing and the wider question of the relationship between textual narrative and spiritual transformation in Christian tradition.

Fear of abandonment by God and desire for admission to his presence interact with one another, as they do throughout the text. God's absence leads the speaker to doubt whether he even believes in God, even loves him at all (II.14.11–14).[5] Yet his awareness of his own desperate desire for God leads him to brush this doubt aside: how could one have such a desire and have no love (II.14.14–16)?

The connection between fear of judgement and love for God becomes increasingly explicit as the narrative unfolds. In *MO* V consideration of the prayers of Jesus during his passion again leads straight back to the fear of everlasting damnation. Jesus only asked forgiveness for those who sinned through ignorance; what of those, such as the speaker himself, who have sinned quite deliberately (V.7–10)? Yet then the pendulum swings back, from fear to hope. The speaker recalls the woman in Luke 7, of whom Jesus said she would be forgiven much because she loved much (V.17.4–5). The speaker continues to dwell on this story, confident that since he too loves much, he may after all be acquitted before the tribunal of the ultimate judge (V.17.7–8).

The text from Luke turns out to be a crucial one, along with Jesus' questioning of Peter at the end of John's Gospel, where Peter is asked three times, 'Do you love me?' This text is introduced at VII.2.9–11, and again the speaker answers the question confidently: 'you know that I want to love you'. Yet is this enough? Anxiety strengthens as, for the first time, the speaker questions whether the mere fact of desiring God is enough for salvation: 'For certainly, O truth, I know that I seek you, but I do not know whether I seek you truly' (VIII.13.11–12). The certainty to which the speaker has so far clung – of his own love for God – now begins to be dismantled. Seeking is not necessarily right seeking. And in *MO* XI, Jesus' questioning of Peter in John 21 returns to haunt him, because Jesus' response to Peter's profession of love was 'Feed my sheep.' 'Pastio gregis probatio est amoris' ('The feeding of the flock is the proof of love'), as the speaker comments (XI.14.10). And yet he is not feeding the sheep, he has abandoned the service of others. How can he then be sure that he loves Jesus?

This thread that we have been tracing through the text is finally wound up in *MO* XII. Today, the speaker asserts, is the decisive day, when he create those whom he knew would be tormented eternally, William rounds the section off with the brutal observation: 'Unless a debtor is hanged, the person whose debt is forgiven is less grateful'.[7] And William's response to such glimpses into the abyss of divine justice is the same as Augustine's: we can only acknowledge and adore God's unfathomable ways.[8]

William held a theology of grace and predestination, then, which reflects in its essential outlines the thought and the concerns of the later Augustine. Yet while Augustine categorically denied that one could know whether or not one were among the elect, William's approach in his more formal theological writings is complex.[9] As we might expect from the previous section, he suggests that we can confirm that we are among the elect by examining our hearts for traces of the love of God.[10] The mere desire that Christ should dwell in the self, indeed the mere fear that he may not, is already a form of love, and therefore already a guarantee that the self is loved.[11] Yet consistently with the *MO*, this does not seem to be enough to bring the deep conviction of salvation that the believer desires.

William stresses that the deep certainty that we are God's children arises from the indwelling of the Holy Spirit while nonetheless suggesting this witness is only experienced at certain times.[12] The very end of the work of grace is the conferring upon the believer of the knowledge that he is the recipient of grace. This knowledge is not coextensive with the entire operation of grace, but rather represents its point of culmination. The awareness of grace is the last link in a chain of divine action that stretches back to eternity.[13] But it is not a possession, or an unchanging condition. The moment of certainty is a point towards which we strive, in which we find momentary rest and from which we then depart to strive again.

Hence the shape of the narrative that the *MO* presents for the appropriation of the reader. The speaker, throughout the entire course of the text, searches for the assurance of a salvation determined by unknowable decree; now despairing, now confident, now unsure, but always looking to his own love for God as the token of that predestined salvation. Finally, when every approach seems inconclusive, there is a sudden disclosure, and the assurance of love is found. Yet no sooner is it found the oscillation of desire which has to contain incompletion. 'Whoever wants to have here all those things that are to be had there shows that he does not have faith'.[16] Faith means acquiescing in a deferral of the goal of desire, a deferral that will last as long as life itself. We are to be perpetually beginning, never arriving. In the *Ep. ad fratres* William says of the progression of love, 'In these matters, when one has finished, then one begins, because there is no full perfection of them in this life'.[17] And he confesses of himself in the *Enigma fidei*, 'in this have I grown old, and I have not yet begun'.[18]

There is also a second major point of difference between the narratives of spiritual transformation in William and in Bunyan. The deepest sense of release from anxiety in William's text arises not in the context of a solitary facing of Christ, as happens suddenly to Bunyan after years of heart-searching as he walks alone through a field,[19] but from the awareness of love for other Christians, who also love God, because they love God and seek to follow in the way of Jesus Christ. Perhaps this represents a distinctive, and indeed decisive, Cistercian note in William's Augustinian narrative.[20]

Finally, it is worth noting that although the MO is among the most widely available of William's works today in English, there is only one surviving Latin manuscript, suggesting it failed to strike much of a chord with his contemporaries or his successors.[21] Indeed, there are few parallels for the creation of narrative in response to Augustinian anxiety between William and the seventeenth century.[22] Contrast the tremendous popularity not only of *Pilgrim's Progress* in its own time but also of properly autobiographical writings from the same period that recount the agonizing search for assurance of salvation.[23] Why that should be is another, and most important, story.

Notes

1   Wolfgang Iser, *The Implied Reader: Patterns of Communication in Prose Fiction from Bunyan to Beckett* (Baltimore: Johns Hopkins University Press, 1974), 18; cf. 26.

18 *Enigma fidei* 24.
19 John Bunyan, *Grace Abounding with Other Spiritual Autobiographies*, ed. John Stachniewski and Anita Pacheco (Oxford: Oxford University Press, 1998), paragraphs 183–89 (66–67).
20 Caroline Walker Bynum, *Jesus as Mother: Studies in the Spirituality of the High Middle Ages* (Berkeley: University of California Press, 1982), chapter 2, 'The Cistercian Conception of Community'.
21 William is represented in the Penguin Classics volume, *The Cistercian World: Monastic Writings of the Twelfth Century*, trans. and ed. Pauline Matarasso (London: Penguin Books, 1993), solely by three of the *MO* (107–24).
22 I have considered one comparable example from later in the twelfth century in 'Adam of Dryburgh and the Augustinian Tradition', *Revue des Études Augustiniennes* 43 (1997): 339–47.
23 Cf. David Booy, *Personal Disclosures: An Anthology of Self-writings from the Seventeenth Century* (Aldershot: Ashgate 2002).

Bibliography

Booy, David. *Personal Disclosures: An Anthology of Self-writings from the Seventeenth Century*. Aldershot: Ashgate, 2002.

Bynum, Caroline Walker. *Jesus as Mother: Studies in the Spirituality of the High Middle Ages*. Berkeley: University of California Press, 1982.

Iser, Wolfgang. *The Implied Reader: Patterns of Communication in Prose Fiction from Bunyan to Beckett*. Baltimore: Johns Hopkins University Press, 1974.

Matarasso, Pauline, trans. and ed. *The Cistercian World: Monastic Writings of the Twelfth Century*. London: Penguin Books, 1993.

Stachniewski, John, and Anita Pacheco, eds. *Grace Abounding with Other Spiritual Autobiographies*. Oxford: Oxford University Press, 1998.

Tugwell, Simon. *Ways of Imperfection: An Exploration of Christian Spirituality*. Springfield, IL: Templegate, 1985.

William of St Thierry. *Disputatio adversus Petrum Abaelardum* (PL 180: 249–82).

—*Exposé sur le Cantique des cantiques*, edited by J. M. Déchanet. SC 82. Paris: Éditions du Cerf, 1975.

—*Expositio super Epistolam ad Romanos*, edited by Paul Verdeyen. CCCM LXXXVI. Turnhout: Brepols, 1989.

—*Lettre aux frères de Mont-Dieu (Lettre d'or)*, edited by J. M. Déchanet. SC 223. Paris: Éditions du Cerf, 1975.

8

Attitudes to the Body in Fourteenth-century English Mystical Literature

STEFAN REYNOLDS

In the last fifty years the disciplines of history and spirituality have worked closely together. If one compares the work of Evelyn Underhill and that of Bernard McGinn one can appreciate how much the study of mystical texts has moved towards seeing them in historical context and not simply as a deposit of an eternal truth. New approaches in history also have had their influence on the interpretation of spirituality. The Marxist critique of a history of the elite, for example, has had its echo in liberation theology and a new appreciation of the writings and experience of women has motivated and informed much feminist theology. One of the latest aspects of the human story to be recovered and have a cross-disciplinary influence is the history of the body. The term 'Body History' was coined by Ivan Illich in *Medical Nemesis* in 1975 and *Gender* 1983.[1] This prophetic voice on the edge of the Church had its echo right in the centre when John Paul II titled his 1979–84 General Audiences 'A Theology of the Body'.[2] Both agreed that by treating the body as merely biological we miss its anthropological and theological significance. Illich lays the charge at the materialism of eighteenth-century medical practice and the separation of social roles from gender; John Paul saw it in the idealism of eighteenth-century morality which separates ethical practice from natural law.

The significance of the body in human and divine experience has

At this time I saw a body lying on the earth, a body which looked dismal and ugly, without shape or form as if it were a swollen and heaving mass of stinking mire. And suddenly out of this body there sprang a very beautiful creature, a little child perfectly shaped and formed, quick and bright, whiter than a lily, which glided swiftly up into heaven. And the swelling of the body represents the great sinfulness of our mortal flesh and the smallness of the child represents the chaste purity of the soul. And I thought, 'None of the beauty of this child remains with the body, nor does any of this body's filth cling to the child.'[3]

To read Julian's reference to 'the wretchedness of the body' as an expression of body–soul dualism would be to read it outside of the context of her message which consistently challenges such an anthropology. This passage can be read within a body-history perspective as dealing with sickness.[4] So too the consolatory message of her *Showings*, famously that 'All will be well'. The plague was felt psychologically as a punishment from God. Julian's revelations specifically reveal Divine compassion and it is in reaction to a tendency to split from the body after a traumatic experience that she affirms God's action and grace within sensuality. The above passage must be read in terms of the lesson that is drawn from it that 'it is more blessed for man to be taken from suffering than for suffering to be taken from man; for if pain is taken from us it may return'. In other words, she attempts to give guidance to those who, despite prayers for God's intervention and healing, had seen or lived with people who died of the plague. The lesson highlights the salvific value of death, not as a punishment but as a permanent release from the suffering inherent in bodily life. The corruptibility of the flesh that leads to death is seen not as God's punishment but as part of God's compassionate action. Julian identifies God's action through the experience of the body. This approach goes hand in hand with an emphasis on the psycho-somatic unity of the human person.[5]

The other approach to the body in the face of trauma is to dis-identify with it so that attention is put on the soul. This 'dis-identifying' with bodily experience, in the form of sickness or of psycho-physical consolation, the contemplative relates to physical experience and the role it plays in spiritual transformation is thus indicative of their stage of progress on the path. The body is the mirror of the soul; where it receives consolation this is because the new convert needs reassurance; where it is tested and mortified this is due to the residue of the soul's sinful disposition; where it enters into rest this is because the soul is no longer swayed by the vicissitudes of the carnal nature. All along the path there is a non-duality of body and soul, for example he says 'solitude in the body greatly helps toward solitude of soul'.[9] Both the feeling of grace in the body and the stripping of that feeling are preparatory for an integration of the body in the stability of the spirit, so that, as Hilton says, 'the body is like nothing but an instrument and trumpet of the soul'.[10]

The difference from Julian lies in Hilton's emphasis on the leadership of the soul. Julian allows bodily experience as a way in to contemplation. In a way similar to much women's mysticism of her time the body becomes the locus of the Divine–human encounter.[11] Contemplation is not understood as dependent on the transcendence of corporal perception. For Hilton the body has a role to play in ascetic formation, but in the further stages of the spiritual path it no longer influences the soul's state. In contemplation, as Hilton understands it, the body finds a new role, mirroring and expressing outwardly the action of grace in the soul.

My next examples come from the writings of Richard Rolle and *The Cloud*. Middle English mysticism is the fruit of the meeting of affective spirituality centred on the humanity of Christ and the apophatic approach of imageless prayer. The former emphasized a bodily imitation of Christ, the latter negated the physical and the historical in its concern for direct relation with God. This can be clearly seen by comparing the attitude to the body in these two writers. Rolle famously expressed his psycho-physical experiences very literally in terms of the senses. For example he writes of his experience of 'calor':

I cannot tell you how surprised I was the first time I felt my heart begin to warm. It was a real warmth too, not imaginary, and it felt as if it were actually on fire.[12]

Truly Christ had ay [always] the contemplation of God, but never the withdrawing from bodily governance. Therefore it is diverse to be rapt by love in the feeling of the flesh, and to be rapt from bodily feeling to a joyful or dreadful sight. I think that it is better to be rapt in the flesh.

Rolle sees rapture as a realized eschatology. Christ had the beatific vision without loss of his senses and in rapture we anticipate the future glorification of our own bodies. This may reflect the scholastic debates at that time over the beatific vision which was both dependent on the separation of body and soul at death and yet could be fully enjoyed only with their reconciliation in the general resurrection.[15]

The difference with *The Cloud* is not just over Rolle's rhetorical use of metaphor but also his hinting at the possibility of a foretaste of bodily resurrection in this life. For the author of *The Cloud* there is no 'rapture in the flesh'. In chapter 59 he makes a distinction between our bodies now and our resurrected bodies after the day of judgement, when 'we shall be so rarefied in our body-and-soul, that we shall be able to go physically wherever we will as swiftly as we can now go anywhere in thought', but now our bodies cannot go where our spirit goes.[16] The term 'body-and-soul' is written as one word by the author implying that after the day of judgement they will be one. In chapter 58 he says that Christ's 'body is inseparably united to his soul', but this is the case for us only after the day of judgement. He counters an argument that may well have derived from Rolle:

If you are going to refer me to our Lord's Ascension, and say that it must have physical significance for us as well as spiritual, seeing that it was a physical body that ascended, and he is true God and true man, my answer is that he had been dead, and then had been clothed with immortality; and so shall we be at the day of judgement. . . . But at the present time you cannot go to heaven physically, but only spiritually. And it is so really spiritual that it is not physical at all.

example. But no one can do that but God . . . so leave such error alone, it cannot be so.[22]

It is clear that there is an important debate among the English mystics on the relation of the spiritual senses to their corporeal counterparts. Are they related metaphorically or as a single sensorium which can be deployed either heavenward or earthward? The affective spirituality of Rolle and Julian expresses a bodily encounter with Christ respectively through psycho-physical consolation or sickness. Those more influenced by the apophatic tradition are concerned that the criteria for contemplation is not defined by issues such as posture, health, bodily comfort or discomfort. Even spatial metaphors like that of interiority and ascent are criticized if they are read in terms of the body. There is always a danger, the author of *The Cloud* says, of reading spiritual things physically and physical things spiritually. However *The Cloud* and Hilton's negation of the body–soul continuum is not a neglect of the body per se but part of a dialectic that uses the body as a foil to direct attention towards what is truly spiritual. The body is seen as distinct from the soul but still an integral and eternal part of the human person. The body is seen as a way of encountering Christ. Rolle bases his mysticism on the felt sense of God's presence; those writing after the plague give meaning to sensual desolation. All see bodily asceticism as playing only a preparatory role in the spiritual path. The soul influences the body and not vice versa. Some like Julian go so far as to see the whole purpose of Christian life as the integration of sensuality. In both their common ground and their variety, these perspectives of the body help to shed much light on the concerns of Middle English mysticism.

Notes

1 Ivan Illich, *Limits to Medicine: Medical Nemesis* (London: Calder & Boyars, 1975); id—, *Gender* (New York: Pantheon, 1983).
2 John Paul II, *Man and Woman He Created Them: A Theology of the Body* (Boston: Pauline Books, 2006).

9

Transformation in the Carmelite Rule

MICHAEL PLATTIG, O.CARM

An essential characteristic of spiritual life in the Judaeo-Christian tradition is that it describes a historical or rather biographical development. Christian spirituality is characterized by concepts such as development, growth, maturation, progression, advance, pilgrimage, ascent, dynamics and transformation. Various images and comparisons, various systematizations to describe this process of transformation, are to be found in the course of history.

A feature they all have in common is the description of a positive development in the sense of personal improvement or rather in the sense of intensification of personal encounters with God. This is not a matter of smooth, ever-ascending biographies. On the contrary, breaks, leaps and bounds, detours and crises necessarily form part of the Christian concept of growth, for they are often just the impetus towards the next step in the maturation process.[1] The guide on this way, as with all designs of Christian spirituality, is God Himself, or rather the Holy Spirit.[2]

Various sets of criteria have been developed in the history of the discernment of spirits to characterize and distinguish the growth guided by God's good Spirit. Describing them would be beyond the scope and object of this chapter. The interesting aspect in the present context of Carmelite spirituality is the characterization of Christian growth as a occupied. It is here that I meet myself in the raw. A great place of purification.

(Whelan 2004:76)

Along with the eremitical tradition it is this conviction which underlies chapter 6 of the Carmelite Rule that reads: 'Next, each one of you is to have a separate cell . . .'. It is the monk's own cell as a sphere of retreat, of solitude and the dialogue with God to which the Carmelite Rule attaches decisive importance. As chapter 10 of the Rule stresses, every Carmelite is supposed to be found in his cell at any time, unless he is busy completing a task in accordance with the Rule. The most important site of spiritual life in Carmel is the cell; it becomes the place of self-knowledge and the knowledge of God and thus the realm of spiritual development or transformation:

The eremitical dimension of Carmel demands that we do everything else out of our experience of the cell. . . . We carry our inner stillness into all aspects of our life and we return to the cell frequently for the refreshment of our stillness.

(Whelan 2004:77)

SILENCE (CHAPTER 21)

The importance of the cell or solitude is closely linked with the emphasis on silence as laid down in chapter 21 of the Rule. Here there exists no contradiction between work and prayer, work is simply a different way of praying, and even of meditating. Being silent while going about one's work is meant to make it easier to experience work as simply another form of prayer.

The Rule also stresses that, according to Isaiah, silence is the way to foster holiness, thus indicating that, far from being a passive or resigned form of silence, this silence is active, as well as an act of creative structuring. In Isaiah 32, the prophet elaborates on this by saying that this means contribute to or create isolation and loneliness, sometimes even becoming the catalyst of breakdowns in communication.

From reading the Carmelite Rule, it is clear that what is meant here is not merely being silent, but rather a very special kind of silence. The Rule implies a silence, or a kind of calmness, which is anchored in the experience of being sustained by the Lord. Not only is this silence based on trust, or faith, in God: the Lord is also its ultimate goal. Discovering the proper balance between words and silence in order to seek the Lord, and, through His grace, to ultimately find Him, is the goal of monastic life, which in the prologue to the Rule is described as *a life of allegiance to Jesus Christ*.

Another characteristic of silence is its relationship to the community in which it is practised: first, out of fraternal consideration (in order not to disturb others during the night), and also out of respect for them (in order not to slander them), and, moreover, as an expression of each member of the community's being focused on the Lord throughout the day.

Thus, what is meant is a silence which is nourished by relationship and which serves to establish and foster it. This kind of silence is not a matter of finding the time or leisure for it or of knowing a particular technique; it is a question of being related to and being transformed by God. The Carmelite Rule teaches silence in the service of one's fellow human beings and God. It means finding the proper place of words in these relationships and taking cognizance of the fact that words can hurt and kill and learning the right balance between times of talking and times of silence.

Talking occupies space. Through talking, people try to get attention and to make others interested in their opinion. Silence, however, creates space for the opinion of others, for the Word of God. Silence allows respect for others to shine forth, not only refraining from saying negative things about them, but also having faith that they have something important to say, that their opinion is worth listening to.

A healthy sense of self-confidence is crucial, an awareness which knows its own value and limits and therefore will always talk when it is time to talk and be silent when it is time to be silent. A person who is in the process of transformation becomes more and more at peace with him or herself and feels secure in God, having no need to be silent out ministry; however, tradition has it that his task is to watch over the spiritual growth of the friars who have been entrusted to his care, to address erroneous attitudes, to prevent all kinds of exaggerations and to encourage and strengthen those who are weary in spiritual life. He is responsible for the so-called 'correctio fraterna' which he is supposed to exercise with humility, i.e. focusing on the welfare of the others.

Similar to the prior, the community has the task to take care both of the individual and the community as a whole. This has been prescribed by chapter 15: 'On Sundays too, or other days if necessary, you should discuss matters of discipline and your spiritual welfare; and on this occasion the indiscretions and failings of the brothers, if any be found at fault, should be lovingly corrected.'

Here the 'correctio fraterna' is explicitly mentioned. Thus these Sunday discussions are primarily intended to explore issues concerning the friars' spiritual welfare. The loving correction also has the aim of challenging and promoting the spiritual growth of the individual friar.

In addition to this, the friars' community is the framework that supports the spiritual development of the individual. It helps to shape and preserve the place that enables spiritual growth. Even if no special effort is made to exchange one's thoughts or discuss matters in detail, it is the community that fundamentally supports the individual by virtue of the mere presence of the friars and the spiritual orientation they share. This means that the community does not only have a corrective function, but above all qualities that support the individual and safeguard the space required.

DISCERNMENT

The end of chapter 24 reads: 'Use discernment, however, the guide of the virtues.' With these words, Albert of Jerusalem concludes his rule for the hermits on Mount Carmel stressing the importance of discernment. What is meant here is establishing the right balance. This interpretation of discernment which we encounter in the Rule being ultimately derived from John Cassian's *Collationes*. Coll. II.2 says:

towards ourselves, others and God. Even these early authoresses and authors warned of the dangers of becoming addicted to experience.

The prudent choice of the right balance, the revelation of one's experience in everyday life: these are the fundamental virtues which the Carmelite Rule has formulated and which have continued to unfold and be interpreted in keeping with the times throughout the history of Carmel. In view of our contemporary situation this prudent kind of practising discernment is needed in our time more than ever.

CONCLUSION

Transformation in the Carmelite tradition takes place in everyday life. This is not about spectacular exercises or ascetic achievements, but rather about a life of allegiance to Jesus Christ (chapter 2 of the Rule) in the sobriety of ordinary life.

The goal of transformation is mystical union with God. The way towards this goal is characterized by the individual's own endeavour to enhance his development in the sense of increasing one's individual freedom, personal independence and social awareness. This is closely linked to the acts of God which shape spiritual growth, go beyond one's own endeavours and ultimately change the individual in dynamic transformation. The tension between one's own actions and the acts of God cannot be transcended, but must be preserved.

The Carmelite Rule offers ample advice and creates networks and institutions intended to promote and support transformation. This also implies the critical instruments of correction and discernment. The advice of this eight-hundred-year-old document is important for the understanding of the necessary instruments to enter the process of transformation also today. The elements described in this chapter were significant at the beginning of the thirteenth century and are still essential for Christian spiritual transformation today: solitude, silence, self-knowledge, self-confidence, meditation on Scripture, *correctio fraterna* and discernment.

10

Teresa of Avila's Transformative Strategies of Embodiment in Meditations on the Song of Songs

PETER TYLER

TERESA AND *THE SONG OF SONGS*

In this chapter I will argue that in her *Meditaciones sobre Los Cantares (Meditations on the Song of Songs*[1]), a commentary on the sensual Hebrew poem the Song of Songs, Teresa of Avila employs a style of writing she has learned from Francisco de Osuna to develop what can be called an 'embodied mystical strategy'. I will begin by reviewing some of the terms used by Teresa before looking at how she borrows from de Osuna before discussing her linguistic strategies in *Meditations*.

As Kavanaugh and Rodriguez make clear in their introduction to their translation of Teresa's works, it is unclear how Teresa would have had access to a translation of this text into the vernacular. Although the Council of Trent had not forbidden the use of scriptures in the vernacular to lay people, the Valdés Indices of 1551, 1554 and 1559 did, especially for 'idiots and *mujercillas*'.[2]

Green (1989), following writers such as Swietlicki (1986), suggests that Teresa had been shown Luis de León's translation of the Song of Songs into the vernacular (for which he was ultimately arrested by the Inquisition) by Martín Gutiérrez (Green 1989:114).[3] On the will respond to. The words themselves are ambiguous and Teresa's use of them opens up what might be called an 'epistemology of delight' in her exploration of the supernatural and mystical. In her use of the erotic and spiritual – the blending of *eros* and *agape*, as well as the human and divine – the key style and tone is *ambiguity*. Let us review these terms.

Gusto[4] is a favourite of Teresa's. Despite attempts to 'tidy up' her prose, both Peers (CW) and Kavanaugh and Rodriguez (CW) convey something of the ambiguity in their translations. In all the word appears one hundred and eighty-five times in her works, fifty-two in the *El Libro de La Vida* (*The Book of the Life*), twenty in *El Libro de Las Fundaciones* (*The Book of the Foundations*), nineteen and twenty-two in *El Camino de Perfección* (*The Way of Perfection*) Valladolid and Escorial codices respectively, thirty-two in the *Las Moradas* (*The Interior Castle*) and thirty-three in *Meditations*. As her writing and style evolves so does her subtlety and use of the word.

The term first appears in chapter 3 of the *Life* where Teresa contrasts her new life in the Augustinian convent of Santa María de Gracia with her previous life of sensuality: 'Mirava más el gusto de mi sensualidad y vanidad quo lo bien que me estava a mi alma' ('I looked more to the pleasure of sensuality and vanity than to what was good for my soul' [V:3.2, my translation]). Thus at its earliest appearance *gusto* is associated with the dubious sensual pleasures she has described in the previous two chapters.

Teresa herself was clearly a lady of some sensuality and she found in prayer that it was difficult to reconcile the two 'so inimical to each other' (V:3). At this stage in the *Life*, and in her writing about these experiences, Teresa contrasts the *gustos* and *contentos* with the *mercedes*, the greater 'favours' that the Lord will give her in prayer (V:7.17). Yet already by chapter 8 she talks of the *gustos* 'bestowed by God', and this is one of her first uses of the term as a description of that which occurs in prayer rather than that which is connected purely with the sensual appetites. Of these *gustos* ('delights' [Kavanaugh and Rodriguez CW/V:8.9], 'consolations' [Peers CW/V:8]), as she now begins to call them, she will tell us more later. But she makes clear, and this will be a constant theme throughout her writing, one of the purposes of prayer is *gusto* – delight, sensuality, eight times, almost as many as *gustos*, and *gozos* eighty-two times. Together with *sabor* Teresa frequently uses *deleites* to convey the right mixture of the sensual and spiritual that she hopes to achieve. By these means she seeks to initiate the necessary *transformation of affect* so central to her 'mystical strategy'. Before we look at this in greater detail in *Meditations*, we shall briefly review Teresa's debt to the tradition of *theologia mystica* as manifest in the works of de Osuna and recognize the similarities of their approaches.

STRATEGIES OF EMBODIMENT IN DE OSUNA

We can find a strong precedent for Teresa's approach to affectivity in the writing of Francisco de Osuna, the only spiritual writer, she tells us in *The Book of the Life*, that really helped her as a young woman struggling with the life of the Spirit (V:8). It is a constant theme in Francisco de Osuna's *Tercer Abecedario Espiritual* (*The Third Spiritual Alphabet*, hereafter 'TA' in citations), as we would expect from a writer who begins his treatise with the phrase 'Anden siempre juntamente – la persona y espíritu' ('Always walking together – the person and the spirit') (TA:1.1), in which he emphasizes the importance of what would today be called a 'holistic' approach to the spiritual life where the body and the spirit are given equal respect:

> The meaning of our letter is that wherever you go carry your mind along, for no one should go divided unto himself. Do not allow your body to travel one path, the heart another.
>
> (TA:1.2, see also TA:8.4)

Like Teresa, de Osuna's approach to spirituality is very much an *embodied* one. The primary concern of *The Third Spiritual Alphabet* is the teaching of the prayer of *recogimiento*,[6] so important for Teresa. Yet the theme of the *gustos* and the importance of spiritual desire or yearning is a key theme of the book. Chapter 12 is dedicated almost totally to it: 'No entendiendo, mas gustando, pienses alcanzar reposo' ('Not hearts to the Lord's gift and accept it' (TA:5.3). It is not fanciful to see such passages as speaking to the young Teresa with their affirmation of passion and of the possibility of the integration of the life of the heart with the life of the mind.

THE *MEDITATIONS*

Teresa's *Meditations* present extended meditations on seven lines from the Song of Songs. In chapter 1 of the work, Teresa reflects de Osuna's play on *sabor/saber* in *The Third Spiritual Alphabet* when she writes:

> Oh my daughters! May our Lord give you an understanding or, to put it better, a taste (for there is no other way to understand), of the joy of the soul when it is in this state.[8]

As with de Osuna she emphasizes the *gustar* of the Lord rather than the *entender*. This is made more explicit in chapter 5:

> While the soul is enjoying the delight (*deleite*) which has been described, it seems to be wholly engulfed and protected by a shadow, and, as it were, a cloud of the Divinity, whence come to it certain influences and a dew so delectable (*tan deleitoso*) as to free it imme-diately, and with good reason, from the weariness caused it by the things of the world.

> (C:5.4)[9]

The theme of the necessary connection between the wisdom of the *gustos* in the taste/enjoyment of God and the need for 'unknowing' of the intellect remains throughout *Meditations*. As Howells (2002:88) points out, *Meditations* occupies an important transitional period in Teresa's writings, from the earlier works such as the *Life* where the emphasis is more on union as rapture, to the later works such as *The Interior Castle* where union is expressed more in terms of service to humanity (Howells 2002:86–88).

For Weber, the 'bride' of *The Interior Castle*, both 'concealed and pro-tected' by Teresa's rhetoric, is erotic spirituality itself, so dangerous in open expression in Spain of the 1570s (Weber 1990:118–22). Weber suggests that Teresa deliberately obscures the erotic spirituality of *The Interior Castle* – 'like a bride in the castle' – all the better to protect it from the Inquisition.

Following the arguments of this chapter, I agree with Weber that there is a sensual or erotic side in *The Interior Castle*, as indeed in all her writ-ings. However, Teresa activates the bodily *affectus* for a purpose, and one which is not merely rhetorical, and certainly not hidden. As we have seen from our consideration of *Meditations*, the end of the sensual self-examination of the *affectus* is to engage our embodied selves and so to enliven us to the world, including the realm of our human relationships with each other. The erotic is not an end in itself for Teresa but a delib-erate strategy of affective transformation, making her spirituality more bodily both in its affect and for engagement with the world.

Notes

1 Hereafter 'C' in citations. All translations are by K. Kavanaugh and O. Rodriguez unless stated.
2 Literally 'little women'. A pejorative term. Kavanaugh and Rodriguez (CW:iii.209) suggest various ways in which Teresa could have had knowl-edge of these scriptures including:
   a) She would have read the verses in Latin in the church office.
   b) She may have used a translation from one of the Spanish offices then available.
   c) She may have asked some *letrado* (literally 'learned man') or confessor to translate for her or she may have got the passages from a spiritual book.
3 Although this is disputed by other commentators, e.g. see Howells (2002: 179).
4 Literally 'taste'.
5 Literally 'delights', 'pleasures' and 'tastes' respectively.
6 Literally 'recollection'. An important movement of the spiritual life in late fifteenth- and sixteenth-century Spain.
7 Space does not permit a full treatment of de Osuna's and Gerson's medieval

OTHER WORKS CITED

Deirdre Green, *Gold in the Crucible*. Shaftesbury, UK: Element, 1989.

Edward Howells, *John of the Cross and Teresa of Avila: Mystical Knowing and Selfhood*. New York: Crossroad, 2002.

Francisco de Osuna, *Tercer Abecedario Espiritual de Francisco de Osuna*, ed. S. López Santidrián. Madrid: Biblioteca de Autores Cristianos, 1998.

—*The Third Spiritual Alphabet*, trans. M. Giles. New York: Paulist Press, 1981.

Catherine Swietlicki, *Spanish Christian Cabala*. Columbia: University of Missouri Press, 1986.

Alison Weber, *Teresa of Avila and the Rhetoric of Femininity*. Princeton: Princeton University Press, 1990.

11

From Absurdity to Apophaticism –
Re-reading Samuel Beckett's
Waiting for Godot

DAVID TOREVELL

INTRODUCTION

What I want to do in this chapter is to offer the possibility of reading Beckett's *Waiting for Godot* in a different manner to which it has normally been read, by illustrating what Christian understandings of silence might entail and how these might inform re-interpretations of the play, in an attempt to create some kind of fruitful dialogue between theatre studies and religious studies. I shall do this by concentrating on how Beckett's use of silence and language has more in common with apophatic traditions of spirituality than with the more standard atheistic or absurdist interpretations. It is not without significance that Beckett himself disavowed the label 'theatre of the absurd' when it came to describing his own work.

In offering a hermeneutics of contemplation towards the text, then, I will focus on the apophatic tradition in religion, since it seeks to highlight those impossibly representational features of the religious life, where, according to Pseudo-Dionysius, the experience of the darkness of unknowing becomes a form of the 'brilliance' of truth. This acceptance of unknowing is the most sure path to any authentic knowing, the

the audience and in so doing, allow an epistemology rooted in apophaticism to take hold. In other words, to offer an experience of alterity or Otherness which exhausts any attempt to communicate it adequately by language. One likely consequence of this is that by coming to rest and feeling at home in silence, one begins to listen attentively to that which is revealed by means of a wordless presence. In order to show this, I shall interweave extracts from Philip Gröning's *Into Great Silence* with Beckett's *Waiting for Godot*, in the hope that this inter-textual exercise will offer a clue to the nature and function of silence both texts represent, a silence more conducive to the spirituality of the apophatic and contemplative traditions than to the genre of absurdist theatre.

INTO GREAT SILENCE

The silence 'filmed' in *Into Great Silence* is situated in the Carthusian monastery La Grande Chartreuse, high above Grenoble in the French Alps. Founded in 1084 by Bruno of Cologne, the monastery became known for its strict rules of silence. The opening sequence of the film shows a Carthusian monk kneeling in silent prayer wearing the white robe of his Order. His contemplative posture and movements become responses to the silence, and, with few distractions, he orders his life towards something 'Great', an experience which envelops the self, yet which appears to be felt within the intimacy of the heart. The camera catches the white-clad monk being enveloped by this intimacy of greatness. This is the impact of the film – that the silence experienced is not simply the empty void of no sound, but the presence of something desirously 'Great'. It is at once overpowering and yet its awesomeness resides in its intimacy and gentleness. As McIntosh claims, 'apophasis happens because . . . persons have been drawn so *close* to the mystery'; it is an 'intensifying of desire to such a point that one is left hungering . . .'.[6] In the darkness and silence of the cinema, the audience too are encouraged to respond to such 'Greatness'.

The scriptural passages are not read aloud, but silently, by the monks and the audience, as the film itself becomes a mediated experience of things attentively. Vladimir insists that Estragon should look at the tree so that he might recognize how it has changed since the previous day: 'The tree, look at the tree'.[9] Some lines later he asks Estragon 'Do you not recognise the place?'[10] Exasperated, Estragon replies, 'Recognise! What is there to recognise?'[11] These are times when Estragon cannot see, cannot behold or hear what Vladimir sees and hears or what the audience might see, but he reassures Estragon repeatedly that in the waiting is seeking: 'When you seek you hear'.[12] Vladimir wants to impress upon Estragon that the day before the tree was black and bare, but 'now it's covered with leaves'.[13] The stage directions at the beginning of Act II state that there are four or five leaves on the stage as well as the boots of Estragon and the hat of Lucky. At moments of indecision and restlessness, Estragon himself comments that they should look resolutely to Nature and as they do so, they also learn to look more closely at each other. Beckett writes near the start of Act II that after Vladimir tells Estragon to look at him: 'They look long at each other, recoiling, advancing, their heads on one side, as before a work of art and then they embrace'.[14]

In his early monograph *Proust*, Beckett refers to Schopenhauer's defini-tion of artistic endeavour as the contemplation of the world independently of the principle of reason, a theme echoed in the stage directions towards the end of Act I, where, in a moment, the light suddenly fails and the moon rises gradually at the back, shedding a pale light on the scene. In this contemplative *mise-en-scène*, an open space against which the gestures and movement of the two central characters operate becomes more stark; the influence of Caspar David Friedrich's painting *Two Men Contemplating the Moon* is apparent. At this point, Estragon, with a boot in each hand, goes to the front of the stage, puts them down and contemplates the moon. In the German version, Beckett used the word *Dreckschuhe* (mud shoes) to describe Estragon's boots and in Act II, somewhat self-pityingly, Estragon says how all 'his lousy life' he has 'crawled about in the mud'. The mud and the sky, the body and the mind, the earth and the sky, hell and heaven, downward and upward, are here set not against, but in relation to, each other. The boots are associated with Estragon's more instrumental and pragmatic attitude to life, but always in some kind of dramatic poise to his more contemplative bearing feel than the struggle with boots. 'Calm yourself, calm yourself',[20] says Vladimir to Estragon when he asks him to recognize the place they had been the day before. And later, as they continue to wait they encourage each other to do 'exercises' and 'some deep breathing' in order to calm themselves down.[21]

The unfolding learning of this 'calming' becomes apparent within both characters. At the moment the moon rises towards the close of Act I, to which I have already referred, it is not Vladimir but Estragon who contemplates the moon and whose upward glances call forth a sense of pleasing surprise from Vladimir, indicated by his question, 'What are you doing?'[22] Has Vladimir sufficiently interested him by this stage in the play that he begins to appreciate the importance of learning to see the world in a new way? Or are we recognizing here that the importance of maintaining a contemplative mode of being is never finally forgotten by Vladimir and Estragon? In reply to Vladimir's question 'What are you doing?', Estragon half remembers Percy Bysshe Shelley's poem 'To the Moon', pointing to how the moon must be weary, gazing 'on the likes of us'.[23] There is a self-recognition of their own weakness here, their relentless toing and froing, their sadness and happiness, resolve to go and indecision to remain, their thoughts of suicide coupled with reflections on happiness and the beauty of nature. These are the moments in the play when the moon's silence signifies a protective and consoling presence.

Such silences in Beckett can often bring us back to a 'calming down' and a refusal to give in to the claim that all there is is endless waiting. For there is something beyond and in the silence, in the struggle to make their own language account for the world, its collapse becomes more dramatic, suggesting that intimations of meaning might start to emerge in its downfall. Although at times silence might threaten to swallow everything up, its presence, which separates the lines of the characters, betrays Beckett's attempt to heighten the sense of contemplative space throughout the play. The exchanges between the two central characters invariably come about because they are unable to remain silent; Estragon and Vladimir acknowledge this. They realize knowingly that their words are a mere excuse, a filling in of the time, a refusal to allow silence to work its transformative, if at times beguilingly demanding, presence.

not a way of saying nothing about the divine. Rather, as Turner comments, it is 'the encounter with the failure of what we must say about God to represent God adequately. If talk about God is deficient, this is a discovery made visible within the extending of it into superfluity, into that excess in which it simply collapses under its own weight'.[29] A more disturbing naming of the mystery of waiting turns out to be none other than an idolatrous waiting, a naming too early and too insistent, a naming which names nothing because it claims a name too prematurely. Naming is associated with a detrimental active searching and a rejection of a more passive waiting. As Simone Weil writes, 'Man should do nothing but wait for the good and keep evil away'.[30]

CONCLUSION

Let us end where we began, with lines from Thomas Merton: 'The contemplative has nothing to tell you except . . . that if you dare to penetrate your own silence . . . you will . . . recover the light and capacity to understand what is beyond words and beyond explanations because it is too close to be explained'.[31] This spiritual insight might, as I have tried to suggest, go some way to assisting us in re-reading Beckett's *Waiting for Godot*, not as absurdist theatre, but as a drama of apophatic and hopeful waiting, in which the performance of silence plays a significant part.

Notes

1 Pseudo-Dionysius, *Mystical Theology*, ch. 1, 997B, *The Complete Works* (NY: Paulist Press, 1987), p. 135.
2 See Rachel Muers, *Keeping God's Silence* (Oxford: Blackwell, 2004), especially pp. 10–11.
3 Denys Turner, 'Apophaticism, idolatry and the claims of reason', in O. Davies and D. Turner (eds), *Silence and the Word* (Cambridge: Cambridge University Press, 2008), pp. 11–34 at 18.
4 Thomas Merton, in W. Shannon and C. Bochen (eds), *Thomas Merton: A Life in Letters* (NY: HarperOne, 2008), p. 168.

Bibliography

Samuel Beckett, *Samuel Beckett: The Complete Dramatic Works* (London: Faber & Faber, 2006).

David Cooper, *The Measure of Things: Humanism, Humility, and Mystery* (Oxford: Oxford University Press, 2007).

Philip Gröning, *Into Great Silence* (Soda Pictures, 2006).

Ulrika Maude, *Beckett, Technology and the Body* (Cambridge: Cambridge University Press, 2009).

Mark McIntosh, *Mystical Theology: The Integrity of Spirituality and Theology* (Oxford: Blackwell, 1998).

Rachel Muers, *Keeping God's Silence: Towards a Theological Ethics of Communication* (Oxford: Blackwell, 2004).

Pseudo-Dionysius, *The Complete Works*, trans. Colm Luibheid (NY: Paulist Press, 1987).

William Shannon and Christine Bochen (eds), *Thomas Merton: A Life in Letters* (NY: HarperOne, 2008).

David Steindl-Rast, *Prayer of Recollection* [audio tape] (Kansas City: National Catholic Reporter, 1977).

—*A Listening Heart: The Spirituality of Sacred Sensuousness* (NY: Crossroad, 1999).

Denys Turner, 'Apophaticism, idolatry and the claims of reason', in Oliver Davies and Denys Turner (eds), *Silence and the Word* (Cambridge: Cambridge University Press, 2008), pp. 11–34.

Simone Weil, *Waiting on God* (London: Collins, Fountain Books, 1978).

12

Patrick Kavanagh: Poet of the Transformative Power of the Incarnation

UNA AGNEW, SSL

The Irish poet Patrick Kavanagh (1904–67) was born and reared in the drumlin hills of South County Monaghan in East Ulster. He was the son of a shoemaker, and in 1926 acquired a small farm at 'Shancoduff' which he immortalized in a sonnet by the same name.[1] He was educated at the local two-teacher primary school at Kednaminsha where he received a thorough grounding in the three Rs and an even more rigorous grilling in the Reilly Catechism and Bible History. In his autobiography *The Green Fool*, he writes:

> The most important subject on the curriculum was the catechism. At cramming children with religion our teacher had few equals. For weeks before a religious examination nothing was taught but the catechism; which same has the result of driving all orthodox piety out of me forever.[2]

This nine-year period in primary school (1909–18) was the limit of the poet's formal education. He left school while still in fifth class without progressing into sixth.[3] 'Not promoted' is the remark ironically penned beside the name of Kednaminsha's most famous and undoubtedly most catechesis and with the discovery of intimations of God, not simply 'in the tabernacle', but in the backward places of his Monaghan landscape, has made a significant contribution to Irish theology, although slow to be acknowledged. Showing that he is aware of his untutored approach, he coyly portrays his poet-farmer character Tarry Flynn, who is roundly dismissed by the parish priest, as 'a perfect fool. Yes, he takes on to know things that men have spent years in colleges to learn.'[9] But Kavanagh had intuitive insight into mystery which others may have missed.

There was a lack of optimism in current religious teaching, which may have prompted Kavanagh to salute a God of colour and beauty in the cut-away bogs of rural Ireland. He writes in celebratory tones, at a time when he had recently recovered from lung cancer surgery:

> Green, blue, yellow and red –
> God is down in the swamps and marshes
> Sensational as April and almost incredible
> The flowering of our catharsis.
> A humble scene in a backward place
> Where no one important ever looked
> The raving flowers looked up in the face
> Of the One and the Endless, the Mind that has baulked
> The profoundest of mortals.
>
> ['The One', 1958]

God's lavish beauty and colour are to the forefront of the poet's mind coupled with a delight that a useless 'cut-away bog' could be selected as the divine trysting place with local people. The poet took pains to reinstate the ordinary events of daily life – a kiss, a laugh, a tear – as the context for encounter with God:

> God is in the bits and pieces of Everyday –
> A kiss here a laugh again and sometimes tears
> A pearl necklace around the neck of poverty.
>
> ['The Great Hunger', stanza VI, 1940–42]

for him 'love's doorway to life'. In 1951 he still affirms their capacity to claim immortality for him in the field of letters:

> I cannot die, unless I walk
> Outside these whitethorn hedges
>
> ['Innocence', 1951]

Sheer delight in the plenitude of nature never ceased to move him. God is sacramentally present in an especially healing capacity in the 'leafy-with-love banks' that pour 'redemption' for him and rebaptize him in his calling as poet on the banks of the Grand Canal in 1955 as he recuperated from invasive surgery. Water for him is 'always virginal, / always original, / it washes out Original Sin',[14] a refreshing variation on the Reilly Catechism of his early school days. The all-pervading radiance of God in these fortuitous contexts presents numerous epiphanies of divine life. Kavanagh ends his life by declaring in gratitude: 'It is October over all my life'. He believes that he has completed his mission as a poet, his harvest is secure, and heaven is close to hand. In the wake of all his previous excesses and cantankerousness, all he wants now is 'a life with a shapely form / . . . capable of receiving / With grace, the grace of living.'[15] In retrospect he sees a transformative dynamic at work in his life.

METAPHOR OF EARTH

The origin of Kavanagh's understanding of God's presence in nature grew from a unique personal vision that opened for him 'chance windows of poetry or prayer' in the most mundane situations.[16] Even a rubbish dump is redolent with mystery. His high-voltage imagination creates of this waste ground, 'the garden of the golden apples'; old discarded boots are 'flying sandals' and 'buckets rusty holed with half hung handles' imaginary drums.[17] His most earthy declaration of God's commitment to pitch tent among us must surely be expressed in the lines:

> And Christ will be the green leaves that will come
> At Easter from the sealed and guarded tomb.
>
> ['The Great Hunger', stanza III, 1940–42]

A redemptive trinitarian motif is introduced here with a hint of tentativeness: 'Yet sometimes . . .'. The lines that follow imply a 'knowing' of God and a communion in the dynamism of Trinity that inevitably invades the consciousness of simple, even unworthy people, in tune with the sacredness of earth. The communion implied by Kavanagh in these lines is close to that articulated in the Fourth Gospel, where the invitation is that of organic oneness with the Godhead: 'I am the vine, you are the branches . . . remain in my love' (Jn 15.5-6).

KAVANAGH BLENDS MYSTICAL VISION WITH HUMOUR

As theologian of the commonplace, Kavanagh learns to blend humour with vision. On one occasion he depicts his fictional alter ego Tarry Flynn, sensing the palpable presence of the Holy Ghost in a lush field of turnips.[20] As he cast his eye over the fields, he sensed the Holy Spirit 'taking the bedlam of the little hills and making them into a song'. 'The totality of the scene around him was a miracle'. Sceptical of what he first saw, he verified his vision, noting that 'the little weeds and flowers' had 'God's message in them'. Tarry Flynn hurries home, rapt in mystical thoughts, determined to try out his ideas on his mother: 'The Holy Spirit is on the fields', he says. At this precise point in the narrative, Kavanagh positions the mother 'with one shoe off and her foot on a stool', preparing to pare her corn. The outlandish juxtaposition of earthiness and spirituality is deliberate. The mother, a staunch parishioner, thoroughly compliant with orthodox religion, suggests to her son, whom she considers 'mad', that he attend the forthcoming Redemptorist Mission to 'sort out' his ludicrous vision of seeing 'the Holy something' in the fields. She adds, with relief and a twinkle in her eye, 'she knew there was no madness on her side of the house'. As a prose writer, Kavanagh is now master of the 1950s. He railed at 'the sharp knife of Jansen' that indiscriminately 'cuts all the green branches'. It was as if the whole Irish Christian society as he knew it, like a devastated wasteland, was despoiled of the life-giving sap of genuine Christian faith and ashamed of being human:

> Not sunlight comes in
> But the hot-iron sin
> Branding the shame
> Of a beast in the Name
> Of Christ on the breast
> Of a child of the West.

['Lough Derg', 1942]

Writing in *Kavanagh's Weekly*, he pointed out that if the Irish Church and priests in general took a more realistic approach to human frailty and ended their stance of denial in relation to the human condition – and especially their insistence that 'Holy Ireland' was somehow immune from the excesses of sin – religion would be more healthy. If sin were accepted as commonplace (without complacency), he believed, there might be less of it. In the light of the sorry findings reflected in the recent Ryan Report (May 2009), perhaps Kavanagh's perception of unreality writ large was correct. In the thirteen editions of his newspaper, for which he was editor, feature-writer and resident poet all in one, he took the liberty of expressing views he had long since bottled. Irish priests, he believed,

> should return to real Catholicism, to root their religion in Life, to accept sin as a commonplace of living and to look at it clearly without fear. The ordinary Irish man or woman is taught at school to fly from sin, to shut his eyes to it, to imagine that it does not exist. In other words he is not educated.[22]

He also believed that Irish Catholicism has an over-exalted sense of itself, but in reality tended to be over-sentimental and have shallow roots. 'What is needed', he adds, 'is depth of spirituality and real backbone'.[23]

Kavanagh refers with characteristic irreverence to the so-called

And I had a prayer like a white rose pinned
On the Virgin Mary's blouse.

['A Christmas Childhood', 1940]

No Irish poet has so thoroughly Christianized the Irish landscape as
has Patrick Kavanagh. Hopkins may marvel at a Christ who makes 'O
marvellous new Nazareths in us';[27] Kavanagh ensures that we recall that
our own backyard *is* Bethlehem. A hurrying passer-by exudes the highly
charged expectancy of the moment:

I can't delay now, Jem
Lest I be late for Bethlehem.

['Christmas Eve Remembered', 1939]

While writing in Dublin during the 1940s, in financial straits as usual,
he tries to recover his original sense of wonder at Christmas by putting
himself through the purifying ritual of engaging with the penitential
aspects of 'Advent'.

We have tested and tasted too much, lover!
Through a chink too wide there comes in no wonder.

He gently admonishes his own excesses, in these memorable opening
lines. Slowly, patiently through the span of the double sonnet format, he
restores his soul to a sense of 'spirit-shocking wonder' and surprise when
Christ slips almost unnoticed into his life again with the appearance of
an early spring flower. The austerity of the ascetical process spelt out in
the ritual discarding of needless, inhibiting baggage, becomes ethereally
raised by the weightlessness of the final line:

And Christ comes with a January flower.

To conclude, Kavanagh's understanding of God's presence in nature
brings together the feast of the Incarnation with the approach of renewed
life in spring. Both events confirm for him the Isaian metaphor that

7   Canon Bernard Maguire (1869–1948), former rector of the Irish College at Salamanca, was parish priest of Inniskeen from 1915 until his death. He was a distinguished scholar and renowned for his fine sermons. See Una Agnew, *The Mystical Imagination of Patrick Kavanagh: A Buttonhole in Heaven* (Dublin: Columba Press, 1998), pp. 57–62.

8   'Having Confessed', in Kavanagh, *The Complete Poems*, p. 256.

9   Patrick Kavanagh, *Tarry Flynn* (London: Penguin Books, 1972 reprinted 2000), p. 142.

10 *The Green Fool*, p. 178–79. See Esther de Waal, *A World Made Whole: Rediscovering the Celtic Tradition* (London: Fount/HarperCollins, 1991), pp. 67–98.

11 'Pilgrim Without Petrol', *Standard*, 23 April 1943.

12 'Lough Derg', *The Complete Poems*, pp. 104–24.

13 'A Prayer for Faith', *The Complete Poems*, p. 8.

14 The quotations in this section are taken from poems published in 1958, popularly called 'The Canal Bank Poems' (*The Complete Poems*, pp. 287–301). The corresponding part of the Reilly Catechism is 'Q. What is baptism? A. It is a sacrament which cleanseth us from original sin, maketh us Christian, children of God and of the Church' (Reilly, *A Catechism*, p. 30).

15 'The Self Slaved', *The Complete Poems*, pp. 293–94.

16 'The Great Hunger', stanza XI, *The Complete Poems*, pp. 79–104.

17 Quotations from 'The Long Garden', *Collected Poems* (London: Martin, Brian & O'Keeffe, 1972), pp 74–75

18 Una Agnew, 'Kavanagh's Holy Door', *Sunday Miscellany*, ed. Cliodhna Ni Anluain (Dublin: New Island Press, 2006), pp. 357–60.

19 'April', *The Complete Poems*, p. 20.

20 Patrick Kavanagh, *Tarry Flynn* (novel) (Middlesex: Penguin Books, 1978), pp. 29–30.

21 'The Windhover', in *Gerard Manley Hopkins: Poems and Prose selected by W. H. Gardner* (Middlesex: Penguin Books, 1953), p. 30.

22 'The Light that Fails', in Patrick Kavanagh (ed.), *Kavanagh's Weekly; A Journal of Literature and Politics*, facsimile edition, Vol. I, No. 11 (Newbridge, Ireland: Goldsmith Press), 21 June, 1952, p. 6.

23 'The Light that Fails', p. 6.

24 'Finnegan's Wake', *Kavanagh's Weekly*, Vol. I. No. 5, 10 May, 1952, p. 1.

25 Esther de Waal, *A World Made Whole: Rediscovering the Celtic Tradition* (London: Fount/HarperCollins, 1991), p. 3.

26 There are approximately six Christmas poems extant. Those referred to here are 'A Christmas Childhood' and 'Advent' (*The Complete Poems*, pp. 143 and 124 respectively).

13

Reflexive and Transformative Subjectivity: Authentic Spirituality and a Journey with Incest

MICHAEL O'SULLIVAN, SJ

Christian spirituality as a lived and researched phenomenon enters the world and undergoes change there via human knowing and choosing. This means that the struggle between authenticity and inauthenticity in the knowing and choosing of those who live and study spirituality is the methodological foundation of Christian spirituality. It follows that the struggle to be authentic and the factors affecting it must receive greater attention in the academic discipline of spirituality at the level of spirituality programmes and research. Such attention is necessary if we are to a) revitalize and transform Christian traditions in the context of contemporary challenges, so that they can be sources of transformation as this book suggests, and b) appreciate the methodological value of such revitalization and transformation for the knowing and choosing of those desiring to live a spirituality of authenticity. This chapter is mainly concerned with the latter. I will attend to this struggle concerning an authentic life by analysing the narrative of a Catholic woman who suffered incest in the Netherlands around the beginning of World War II. In order to do so I will first articulate an account of the methodology of human knowing and choosing at a foundational level as the human source of spirituality. I will pay particular attention in the narrative analysis to the methodological

We need therefore to function on the foundation and in the horizon of self-appropriated authenticity in knowing and choosing for the sake of transforming and revitalizing traditions of Christian spirituality for today, because that is the way to a critically real objectivity. We also need to realize that such functioning itself constitutes a spirituality because it involves fidelity to the practices in interiority of attending, inquiring, judging and deciding that give access to beauty, intelligibility, truth, goodness and love. Such spiritual practice can move one to a Christian conversion as is the case, for example, when a person accepts that his or her desire for authenticity is a gifted desire from God for the sake of being able to come into communion with Jesus Christ as the revelation of God's beauty, intelligibility, truth, goodness and love in life. In other instances fidelity to the spiritual practices that are the methodological foundation in subjectivity for reaching objectivity may have recognized implications for how one understands and lives an existing Christian commitment.

The story of Margaret, to which I will now turn, illustrates much of what I have been saying about the human desire for authenticity in subjectivity, how belief directs much of our knowing and choosing, especially during childhood, and how this can lead to good people being deceived by their desire for authenticity. Margaret's story also has implications for our Christian traditions as it will show the necessity of subjecting them to a virus scan in relation to the well-being of women.

MARGARET[1]

Margaret was born in 1926/27. She was about twelve years old when her brother, who was three years older, committed incest with her.[2] This means in the light of what I have said earlier that Margaret was now faced as a growing female child with the need to process her experience of incest with the spiritual practices of attending to data, raising questions, making judgements and taking decisions, including ones about what to believe from her Christian faith, and to do so in the context of a particular historical and cultural milieu, and with an inherent desire to live with integrity and transcendence in virtue of the structured dynamism of that we would end up in hell together, because we'd done something that was absolutely forbidden . . . You always had to be servile, to serve God. Women were totally ignored. But whenever evil enters the picture, it is always mentioned in the same breath with the word 'women' . . . It seemed to me that women were always to blame. They were either bad, or diseased, or possessed by the devil.[4] . . . Women are always portrayed as evil, like Eve, who incites the man to evil. The woman is always the symbol of evil and wickedness.[5]

The view of women as scapegoats that Margaret learned meant that while she was afraid that her brother, also, would lose eternal salvation, she was the one who had been 'the devil's gateway', to use Tertullian's phrase about Eve, and by implication all women.[6] This learned understanding of herself as a woman in the context of a religious worldview with implications for male gender-related violence against women can be regarded as a form of traumatic violence.[7]

Messages learned concerning marriage reinforced the trajectory of her disempowerment as a woman in relation to male violence against women:

A mother sacrificed everything for her children and her husband. Being a good wife was one big sacrifice[8] . . . When the marriage wasn't going well, it was always the wife's fault, because she was supposed to make sure that the husband got what he was entitled to.[9]

The gender role of women in marriage according to this understanding that Margaret learned meant that the good of the male spouse included his right to have sex with his female spouse, who had committed herself to him, whenever he wanted it, irrespective of what she might feel as a person and in her sexuality – if she still knew. The view of the husband here is of someone in the grip of a sexual drive that was not obliged to take account of the fact that he was married to a person, a sexual person endowed with a capacity for responses that could differ from his and entitled to have them respected. If she, on the other hand, did not 'give way' to him,[10] and this undermined the marriage, she would be blamed.

of saving love, as emphasized by Gustavo Gutierrez and Liberation theologians.

Margaret has some sense of Jesus as one who liberates women from oppression. But the oppression he liberates them from is their being bad, diseased, or 'possessed by the devil'.[17] He liberates them from themselves in a way that does not attend to the oppression and violence they may have been suffering as a result of culture, social structure and religious tradition. For example, while she learned about Jesus liberating women from being 'possessed by the devil' in order to cure them,[18] there is no mention of Jesus as the saving love of God expelling the devil from men who were violent to women and in that way curing them both. This is understandable since it is not a biblical theme. However, the biblical story of Jesus stopping men stoning the woman to death who was accused of adultery and brought before Jesus in the Temple is also not mentioned.[19]

The messages Margaret learned concerning, for example, God, sin, keeping rules, being a woman, what was expected of her in marriage, the meaning of loving your neighbour as yourself, and Jesus and women have to be interpreted in the light of the early foundational understanding in her life of what salvation meant. Because she learned and believed that this life was a trial and a test to discover who was worthy of an eternal salvation beyond the grave, that one wrong move could cost her eternal salvation, unless she was able to atone for such presumed wrongdoing, and that God was a frightening God, other messages she received concerning how life was to be lived as a Catholic woman would have been affected by this central one concerning the character of God and the salvation 'he' offered. Given, as well, that her received understanding of salvation did not integrate opposition to male gender-related violence against women as part of the reality of salvation, it is reasonable to hold that the combined effect on her of what she learned and accepted concerning salvation and messages related to it disempowered her in a situation of male gender-related violence against her and greatly added to her trauma. It is also reasonable to presume that the violence of being made vulnerable to male violence through the kind of religious conditioning she experienced was the lot of many other women at the

Notes

1   See Annie Imbens and Ineke Jonker, *Christianity and Incest* (Kent: Burns & Oates, 1992), 54–62.
2   Imbens and Jonker, *Christianity and Incest*, 54 and 56.
3   Imbens and Jonker, *Christianity and Incest*, 54–55.
4   Imbens and Jonker, *Christianity and Incest*, 58.
5   Imbens and Jonker, *Christianity and Incest*, 59.
6   Tertullian, *De Cultu Feminarum*, 1:1.
7   'Traumatic violence, by definition, overwhelms abilities to protect self and others. It renders victims helpless or fearful for their lives . . . Traumatic effects linger long after physical injuries have healed and violent events have come to an end' (Robert W. Grant, 'The Healing of Violence', *Human Development* 23/4 [2002]: 5–7 at 6).
8   Imbens and Jonker, *Christianity and Incest*, 59.
9   Imbens and Jonker, *Christianity and Incest*, 60. Margaret does not mention the household code texts in what she says about marriage, but what she says about marriage reflects the way these texts have been transmitted and received for so long in the Christian community. It is reasonable to suppose, therefore, that these texts may have helped form the way Christian marriage was understood and lived in her society, but without those concerned being aware of that. The authors of *Christianity and Incest* say as much in pp. 249–59 where they treat texts, prayers, questions and formulas used in Catholic marriage services in the Netherlands from 1947.
10 This phrase appears in Ephesians, a household codes text. The text containing the phrase is offered as a reading for Mass on the Feast of the Holy Family. Some years ago the then Taoiseach (Prime Minister) of Ireland, Albert Reynolds, said, responding to a female politician of another political party in the Dail (Irish parliament), that a problem about women today was that they did not give way. A number of papal statements which would have been influential in Catholic circles and on Margaret's life are also worth noting here. Pius XI, in *Casti Connubii* (*On Chaste Wedlock*), published in December 1930, wrote: 'The same false teachers . . . do not scruple to do away with the honourable and trusting obedience which the woman owes to the man. Many of them even go further and assert that such a subjection of one party to the other is unworthy of human dignity, that the rights of husband and wife are equal.' See *Encylical Letter of Pius XI on Christian Marriage* (London: Catholic Truth Society), 35. Pope Pius XII, in an address to women of 'Catholic-action' on 26 October 1941 said that bearing a child was 'the sanctity of the nuptial bed. This is the loftiness of Christian motherhood. This is the *salvation* of the married woman' (emphasis mine).

14

A Potential for Transformation: Gay Men and the Future of Christian Spirituality

MICHAEL BERNARD KELLY

In some of the most potent phrases in Christian history, the Second Vatican Council proclaimed that the Church shares the 'hopes and joys, grief and anguish' of contemporary women and men, and committed itself to 'engaging in conversation' with them as an 'eloquent proof of its solidarity with, as well as its love and respect for the entire human family with which it is bound up'.[1]

This commitment has proved challenging for the Church, and nowhere more so than in the area I wish to address – the integration of sexuality and spirituality. As scholars and students of the Christian spiritual tradition we share both this commitment and this challenge. If the tradition is not to become simply a museum piece we must bring it into engagement with real people's lives, and we must welcome their wisdom and their questions.

We could be asked, for example, what the spiritual tradition has to offer as the churches struggle, first with seemingly endless revelations of systemic abuse related to sex and power, secondly with the increasing abandonment of the Church by people in the educated societies of the West, so many of whom say that the churches' attitudes to sex have been not only unhelpful but even destructive and abusive, and thirdly, with the most of these celibates were, as we know, writing within a religious culture that barely tolerated any form of sexual pleasure, even within heterosexual marriage.[3] We simply have no mystical voice that comes to us from people who experienced, then reflected upon, and then articulated, spiritualities that joyously, openly embraced sexual, genital, erotic relationships, much less sexual play and pleasure.

What we do have, however, is the kataphatic way. Christianity is – or ought to be – profoundly incarnational. As the author of the First Letter of John puts it:

> Something which has existed since the beginning,
> that we have heard,
> that we have seen with our own eyes;
> that we have touched with our hands:
> the Word, who is life –
> this is our subject
>
> (1 Jn 1.2)[4]

Harvey Egan says that the kataphatic way, also known as the *via affirmativa*, underscores finding God in all things, affirming that 'God can be reached by creatures, images and symbols, because he has manifested himself in creation and salvation history' – and most especially in Christ, 'God's real symbol, the icon of God'.[5] Price says that the kataphatic way 'mediates the transcendent to consciousness through narratives, through dreams, through natural and aesthetic beauty, through the body, and through theory'.[6] This is familiar territory for most Christians. Whether or not we know the terms, all our prayers, rituals, theologies, texts, icons and teachings are part of the kataphatic way. They are expressions of the immanence, the embodied-ness of God in creation, in us, and especially in Christ.

What tends to be missing, however, from most discussions of the kataphatic way, is the ordinary sexual reality of bodies – our own and those of others, and reflection upon our erotic desires, experiences and pleasures. To suggest that erotically enjoying our own bodies and the bodies of other human persons, and deeply entering into our sexual feelings

feeling of being part of everything, not separate at all. I knew that
if I cut a tree, my arm would bleed. And I laughed and I cried and
I run all round the house. I knew just what it was. In fact, when it
happen, you can't miss it. It sort of like you know what, she say,
grinning and rubbing high up on my thigh.

Shug! I say. Oh, she say. God love all them feelings. That's some
of the best stuff God did. And when you know God loves 'em you
enjoys 'em a lot more. You can just relax, go with everything that's
going, and praise God by liking what you like.

Shug's experience here is profoundly incarnational, kataphatic, sacramen-
tal – it is the deeply immanent awareness that opens us to transcendence
and communion. What makes this passage unique is that, unlike so many
other passages in mystical literature, Shug directly relates the experience
to her sexual body-self, as she experiences holy delight in touching herself
erotically, just as she feels holy delight in touching the earth, the trees,
and other people, and all this – *all this* – leads her to praise God.

There is primal grace here – and I believe that we know this at a
level deeper than our doctrinal conditioning. In a recent essay about
studying spirituality in a time of ecosystemic crisis, Mary Frohlich writes
about requiring her students to reconnect with and articulate their own
'profound and poignant encounters with elements of the natural environment'. She adds, in words that I wish to apply to sexual desire and
erotic intimacy, that students generally do not need to be taught about
connection with the Earth; 'rather, they need to have [their own] experience honoured and its significance brought to articulation so that it can
be placed in dialogue with all their other learning'.[15] In a similar way
we know, at a visceral level, that all kinds of sexual desire and pleasure
can, in themselves, be numinous, liberating, ecstatic, holy – but we need
to have this experience honoured, articulated and brought into dialogue
with our religious tradition. Surely the doctrine of the Incarnation
demands this. To encounter the divine through an icon, or a ritual, or a
crafted meditation, but fail to taste the divinity in our erotic encounters
with human persons is to turn away from the mystery of the Word made
flesh, living and dwelling among us. We are called to re-embody and re-

test and to discover for ourselves – and we now know that it is not any particular sexual activity in itself that is the issue, rather it is the quality of relating to oneself and to the other that matters. This simple discovery opens up the possibility of maturely and creatively applying to our sexual lives the fundamental values of Christianity: faith, hope and love, and recognizing that these will find varying expressions in varying lives, and that we are all the richer for that.

This learning has come about in the context of much pain, many mistakes and deep experiences of loss, as well as of bliss.[17] You will have noticed that already, though discussing sex, pleasure and the kataphatic way, I have stressed that gay men have had to defy, or at least lay aside, teachings about our sexuality that we were solemnly taught came from God. To test these teachings, not only with our minds but with our bodies, is to set our feet upon an apophatic way, upon which we take the risk that all our hallowed words, theologies, moral codes, structures of sacred authority, religious life-projects and understandings of ourselves and of God may unravel, and we may find ourselves lost, alone, empty and in the dark.

The apophatic way teaches that God can never accurately be spoken of in terms of what God is, but only through saying what God is not. Anything that is affirmed of God must be immediately 'unsaid' – yet the unsaying does not convey anything of God that can be grasped. God, the Absolute Mystery, is beyond word, concept or image. As Michael Sells has shown, apophatic language is a 'performance' in which saying and unsaying depend on one another, turn back on one another, and, in the profound tension that he calls 'the apophatic moment', there is evoked, fleetingly and unstably, a sense of mystery, of wonderment, of bewilderment 'not outside of, but within, our cultural, religious, theological and philosophical world-views, at the horizon where they point beyond themselves'.[18]

Implicit in what Sells says is the understanding that our worldviews do indeed have horizons where they point beyond themselves. Actually experiencing this is radically unsettling, for those horizons, and the spiritual paths that lead to them, are places where the security and meaning offered by our worldviews collapse. The idea that our words about an apophatic praxis, learning to suspect that beneath any sacred word, image or teaching lay an unknowing that could, perhaps, be glimpsed, but never contained. Even some of our humour emerges from a sharp sense of the need to 'unsay' so much of what is endlessly 'said' by sacred authorities, and from our lived experience of the ludicrousness, and the potential oppressiveness, of humans imagining they have captured the divine.

To turn to the second movement, apophatic awareness itself, as it emerges in our spiritual lives, does its own work of shaking loose our hold on words about God and God's will, drawing us inexorably towards that atheism which 'is a purification of the notion of God',[22] as Simone Weil puts it. When this is happening at the same time, and in the same life as the sexually based apophatic loosening, the result is profoundly disturbing and freeing. Apophatic spiritual awareness merges with apophatic sexual experience, each movement opening to and intensifying the other, drawing us into ever more radical stripping. The apophatic spiritual path of the gay Catholic leaves no place to stand except naked trust, grounded in the truth of our bodies, as well as our souls.

The third movement concerns sexual experience itself, which gradually reveals itself as a dance between presence and emptiness. Excluded from all the religious constructs that claim to give sex meaning or justification or grace, we have had to experience sex just as it is – and hold it up to the light of discernment, and the darkness of mystery. We have learned that the holy immanence in sex, which can be radiant and glorious but also plain and simple, ultimately melts into emptiness – that dark face of divine transcendence which can feel ecstatic and wondrous, but which always remains silent, hidden, unknown. Sex, too, has horizons where it points beyond itself.

Gradually sex, like life, reveals itself as a *limen*, a threshold, where the mystery reveals itself and at the same time withdraws, to use Heidegger's words.[23] In sexual experience, as in spiritual experience, we may touch and be touched, but we can never grasp the mystery, immanent and transcendent, incarnate in every person. We learn this, over time, with every embrace, with every letting go.

One final apophatic movement, which I can mention only briefly as I and the Kataphatic Revisited', *Studies in Formative Spirituality* 11 (1990): 195–201 at 195.

3   See Margaret A. Farley, *Just Love: A Framework for Christian Sexual Ethics* (New York: Continuum, 2008), pp. 37–50 for an historical overview of Christian perspectives and teachings on sex.

4   The Jerusalem Bible, Alexander Jones (ed.) (London: Doubleday, Darton Longman & Todd, 1966), First Letter of St John.

5   Harvey Egan, SJ, 'Christian Apophatic and Kataphatic Mysticisms', *Theological Studies* 39/3 (September 1978): 399–426 at 403.

6   Price, 'Transcendence and Images', p. 196.

7   See for example Gerard Loughlin's discussion of the medieval imagery of the relationship between the apostle John and Jesus in his 'Introduction: The End of Sex', in *Queer Theology: Rethinking the Western Body*, edited by Gerard Loughlin (Oxford: Blackwell, 2007), pp. 1–35, esp. pp. 1–4.

8   Carter Heyward, *Touching Our Strength: The Erotic as Power and the Love of God* (San Francisco: Harper & Row, 1989).

9   See for example, Elizabeth Stuart and Lisa Isherwood, *Introducing Body Theology* (Cleveland: Pilgrim Press, 2000).

10   Marcella Althaus-Reid, *Indecent Theology: Theological Perversion in Sex, Gender and Politics* (London and New York: Routledge, 2001).

11   See for example, Gary Comstock, *Gay Theology without Apology* (Cleveland: Pilgrim Press, 1993).

12   See Gerard Loughlin (ed.), *Queer Theology: Rethinking the Western Body* (Oxford: Blackwell, 2007); also Robert E. Goss, *Queering Christ: Beyond Jesus Acted Up* (Cleveland: Pilgrim Press, 2002).

13   Christopher West, *Theology of the Body Explained: A Commentary on John Paul II's "Gospel of the Body"* (Boston: Pauline Books, 2003).

14   Alice Walker, *The Color Purple* (New York: Washington Square Press, 1982), p. 178.

15   Mary Frohlich, RSCJ, 'Under the Sign of Jonah: Studying Spirituality in a Time of Ecosystemic Crisis', *Journal of the American Academy of Religion* (Spring 2009): 27–45 at 38.

16   Amy Hollywood, *Sensible Ecstasy: Mysticism, Sexual Difference, and the Demands of History* (Chicago and London: University of Chicago Press, 2002), p. 9.

17   For a sustained analysis of the stages of loss faced by gay and lesbian Christians, see Craig O'Neill and Kathleen Ritter, *Coming Out Within: Stages of Spiritual Awakening for Lesbians and Gay Men* (San Francisco: HarperCollins, 1992).

18   Michael Sells, *Mystical Languages of Unsaying* (Chicago: University of Chicago Press, 1994), p. 216.

Details of Contributors

Una Agnew, SSL is Associate Professor Emerita in the Department of Spirituality at the Milltown Institute, Dublin. She is author of *The Mystical Imagination of Patrick Kavanagh: A Buttonhole in Heaven* (Columba Press, 1998).

James Alison is a Catholic theologian, priest, and author currently working as a travelling teacher, lecturer and retreat leader. He is based in Brazil and is the author of several books, most recently *Broken Hearts and New Creations* (Darton, Longman & Todd/Continuum, 2010).

Bernadette Flanagan is the Director of Research at All Hallows College (Dublin City University, Ireland). She organized the first European Conference for the academic study of spirituality and co-edited the papers under the title *With Wisdom Seeking God: The Academic Study of Spirituality* (Peeters, 2008).

Edward Howells is Lecturer in Christian Spirituality and Convenor of the MA in Christian Spirituality at Heythrop College, University of London. His interests lie in the history of Christian mysticism and he is author of *John of the Cross and Teresa of Avila: Mystical Knowing and Selfhood* (Crossroad, 2002).

Stefan Reynolds is a PhD student in medieval English mysticism at Heythrop College, University of London. He is administrator of the Institute of Religion, Ethics and Public Life at Heythrop College.

David Torevell is Associate Professor in the Department of Theology, Philosophy and Religious Studies at Liverpool Hope University. His research interests include theology and the arts, contemplative theology and worship. His most recent monograph is *Liturgy and the Beauty of the Unknown: Another Place* (Ashgate, 2007).

Peter Tyler is Senior Lecturer and Programme Director in Pastoral Theology at St Mary's University College, Twickenham, London. His *John of the Cross: Outstanding Christian Thinker* is published by Continuum (2010).

Jeremy Worthen is the Principal of the South East Institute for Theological Education and is also an Honorary Theological Canon and Prebend of Chichester Cathedral. His most recent publication is *The Internal Foe: Judaism and Anti-Judaism in the Shaping of Christian Theology* (Cambridge Scholars, 2009).

Index

199